A Highlander Goes to War

A Highlander
Goes to War
A Memoir 1939–46

Peter Grant

The Pentland Press
Edinburgh – Cambridge – Durham – USA

First published in 1995 by
The Pentland Press Ltd
1 Hutton Close,
South Church
Bishop Auckland
Durham

ISBN 1-85821-330-4

Typeset by Carnegie Publishing, 18 Maynard St, Preston
Printed and bound in Great Britain by Bookcraft (Bath) Ltd.

To my granddaughters
Gillian and Fiona in the
hope that they themselves
will never be disturbed by war.

Contents

Foreword

I first met Peter Grant in a Yorkshire mining town in the spring of 1941. We were both posted, as newly commissioned Second Lieutenants, to the 1st Battalion of The Queen's Own Cameron Highlanders, an historic unit, laden with battle honours, which had been mauled at Dunkirk and was being restored to strength by local drafts of wiry Yorkshiremen and a motley selection of wartime officers converted as rapidly as possible from civilian life by the stern regimens of boot camps and Officer Cadet Training Units.

To Peter, the Camerons were his home regiment, his birth place of Drumnadrochit on the shore of Loch Ness being close to Inverness, the regimental headquarters. To me, a city boy from Glasgow, Peter was the archetypal Highlander, calm, strong, articulate and humorous. Enfolded in the camaraderie of our contemporaries, mostly Scottish, he and I were to soldier together for the next four and a half years, experiencing both the traumas of war and the strains of army life for which we wartime soldiers were ill-prepared.

We had joined up to defend our homeland against a threatened invasion and to assist the restoration of freedom in lands enslaved by the Nazi regime. Instead we found ourselves in a strange and unimaginable war, flung into mortal combat against opponents and in an environment which were totally alien. This was a test of character, to which Peter, as those reading between the lines of his modest narrative will perceive, responded in an exemplary manner.

In the long, weary months of training; in the boredom of disciplined idleness; in the close confinement of two months on a troopship; in the prisonlike exile of remote camps in India; in the high drama of close proximity battle, Peter was always *reliable*, an under-rated quality which becomes a pearl beyond price in times of danger and stress.

In addition to having an even temperament, Peter is good fun and good company. As the mess teetotaller, whose duty was to assist some of his fellow officers to bed, I was uniquely placed to observe Peter's remarkable imperviousness to any visible effect of alcoholic consumption. I was also privileged to appreciate a more memorable talent – his melodious singing voice. His rich repertoire of Scottish songs was much in demand on both formal and informal occasions. His rendering of 'The March of the Cameron Men' articulated many poignant moments in our long saga of comradeship. On tropical nights on the upper deck of our troopship, a group of us would spend half the night singing, learning new songs from one another. The Jocks were not great singers (except when they were really miserable), but they were sentimental listeners, and Peter's singing was often a balm in times of despondency.

Implicit in Peter's account of his wartime adventures is his egalitarian relationship with those under his command, affectionately limned in the numerous anecdotes about his batman. A natural, but not flamboyant, leader, Peter was a pioneer in the much needed democratization of the wartime army and his leadership was recognized by his peers and the Commanding Officer of the Battalion in awarding him the key responsibilities of signals officer and adjutant.

After the bizarre interruption of 1939 to 1945, when we lived together in a close community second only to that of a family, we all – those who survived – went our different ways. I was abroad for twenty years after the war, out of touch with all but two of my wartime friends. My first contact with the Camerons after my return was at the annual Kohima reunion held in York, only a few miles from Thorne, the mining town where Peter and I had first met. And there at the reunion, loyal to tradition and comradeship (I doubt if he has missed one in fifty years) was Peter, imperturbable as ever, his pawky humour intact and somehow ageless, as he has remained into the contemplative years, when we think more often of the dead; yearn more often for shared memories of those who are still with us; and hope that we can pass to the next, and next after the next, generations something of the vividness, the clarity, the never-to-be- repeated certainties of these years of exotic exile from the pattern of peaceful living.

Now Peter has written his story of these distant years, and I suppose I am one of the small and dwindling number of those qualified to appraise it. It is a modest and honest account of one man's part in an extraordinary time when individual experience was dwarfed by the immensity of global conflict. For few was this more true than British troops socially, culturally and geographically isolated in India and Burma for four years. Happenstance witnesses to the end of the Empire (an eclipse more visible to us than those on the major stages of Europe and the Pacific), we could justifiably ask what earthly reason there was for us to be there. The answer to this question about a war so strange in its locale, so personal in its style of combat, so self-absorbed in its meaningless mutual slaughter, can only be sought in the writings of those who were there, to which *A Highlander Goes to War* is an honourable addition.

Gordon Graham
September 1995

Prologue

These memoirs of the Second World War encapsulate what millions of participants have talked about over the years, recollecting what happened to them during that great episode in world history. I have put these experiences into the written word, and claim no more than that they are memoirs, hopefully to entertain and amuse, and maybe to enlighten those who were there and perhaps even those that were not.

Chapter One

On that fateful day, 3 September 1939, I was in Edinburgh, staying with my brother, who was a veterinary student. I normally lived in Fife where I had secured my first teaching post some three years before.

The weekend visit to the city where I graduated was chiefly a courting occasion, but on this occasion my fiancée was not in residence. She too was a teacher and with the threat of war teachers and schoolchildren had been evacuated to the country, some days prior. In one of the great transportation achievements of the time, she found herself in Forres with her class. Local residents took the children and she, too, was found a suitable billet, with one or more colleagues. However, her sister was in Edinburgh for the weekend and on the Sunday morning my brother and she accompanied me to visit her boyfriend, Billy, in a nearby residential area of the city. There was clearly tension in the air, and excitement too, as we switched on the wireless to listen to a broadcast by the Prime Minister, Neville Chamberlain.

At 11 a.m. the cadaverous voice of the Premier came over the air. The message was that Herr Hitler, the German Chancellor, had ordered the invasion of Poland and in accordance with our pledge to that country we, the British people, were now at war with Germany. We were all stunned by the news, for we all knew that the tenor of our lives, careers and hopes for the future were all shattered.

We were all in our early twenties, and would inevitably be called up to the forces.

As we talked, suddenly the air was rent by the wail of the air raid siren. Soon, there were men wearing gas masks on their faces, on the street, telling people to take cover. There was no smell of gas, but our host was taking no chances so we all followed him into a cupboard below the stairs. From time to time we would venture out to see what was happening, and at last, when it appeared there was nothing doing, we emerged, to continue our normal activities as usual.

In the weeks and months ahead there was little to report on the military front. The opposing armies confronted each other from defensive positions along the so-called Maginot line, built by the French and reputed to be impregnable. British formations were once again in France and Belgium.

For some years prior to this, I had been a member of the Edinburgh University Officers' Training Corps. Shortly after the outbreak of war I received a communication from the War Office to the effect that the OTC would be suspended for the duration of hostilities and that in due course I would be called up for service in the Royal Fusiliers, prior to receiving a commission. For I was, by now, in possession of the Qualifying Certificates A and B: the latter, together with a university degree, entitled the holder to a commission in forces of Great Britain or Canada.

I heard no more from that quarter and resumed my normal teaching duties. However, early in 1940, the Government decided to form a home defence force, to be known as the Local Defence Volunteers, to minimize the threat of invasion from Nazi Germany. There was an immediate rush to join and I was one of those applying. The initial organization of this force was in the hands of the Police, but a military structure was necessary. The locality where I lived had few potential NCOs or officers because the menfolk were mainly railway workers, miners or farmers and had little experience of military ways. So it was that within a few days I was visited by the Chief of Police and asked if I was prepared to take command of this body of men, which would provisionally be called the Thornton Platoon, and at that time would muster some 150 volunteers. I accepted the honour, with the usual reservations, and promised to do my best, but warned him not to expect too much.

There was no equipment available, but brassards, with LDV letters emblazoned on them, to be worn on the arm. An office was established in the centre of the village, and presently all the men would come to a parade and to meet me. A nominal roll was called, and an address was given by the area commander. With the good wishes of the top brass and every assurance of support, the Thornton Platoon LDV was established and on its way to defend its country.

My responsibility was quite considerable, for I was playing rugby for the Howe o' Fife RC and acted as its trainer, but with lots of help from the local TA and the Regular Army itself, a measure of discipline and drill took over and soon I was able to appoint a sergeant and NCOs.

Until rifles were available we used broom handles or wooden imitations. One day, however, a number of boxes full of rifles arrived, together with a substantial supply of ammunition. The rifles were new and Canadian in manufacture and heavily greased. The cleaning of these weapons was a major task but when it had been completed each man was the proud possessor of a rifle and 50 rounds of ammunition.

The office became the HQ, and two sentries were posted in the evenings. The sentries had instructions to challenge anyone approaching. All went well until the pictures came out at 10 o' clock. The women came laughing and chattering up the road. The sentry shouted, 'Halt! Who goes there?' The response was to be expected. 'Ye ken fine, Willie, it's me,' and carried on walking home. The sentries gave chase and everyone ran, amid screams and hoots of laughter. Finally the sentries had to return to their posts disconsolately.

This, of course, was evening and weekend work. My day job was teaching at Sinclairtown, in Kirkcaldy. From my classroom window I had a view of the Firth of Forth. One day there was tremendous activity in the air over the Firth. Then, to our consternation, there was the sound of explosions. We then saw planes, including what we now recognized as German bombers. We were witnessing the first air raid on the Forth Bridge. The British fighters were weaving and dodging the larger aircraft that were trying to disrupt the north–south rail communications of the country. The German planes had failed to record a hit and were pursued out to sea by the fighters, who turned out to be an auxiliary formation of part-time airmen from the Lothian area.

The weekends were now given over to field training – searching woods and thickets for possible parachute landings. We obtained the raw materials for making 'Molotov Cocktails', which we made, and we practised ourselves in the use of them. There was, of course, within the unit a tremendous source of technical know-how in the use of explosives and other nasty things which could be used against an enemy.

Badges appeared on caps and, before long, by reason of the natural propensity of the Scot for soldiering, a very reasonable body of volunteers was ready for inspection by the District Commander, who was fulsome in expressing his pleasure at their efficiency and soldiery turn-out on parade.

Throughout the summer of 1940, the platoon reacted quickly to the alarms and excursions; the inevitable echoes of the terrible events taking place in Europe which culminated with the defeat of the allied forces in France, followed by the miraculous escape of the British Army from the beaches of Dunkirk. We were now an embattled island and the men of the LDV had to play a very positive part in the defence of the country. The battle was now being brought to our own shores with ever-mounting attacks from the air, by day and by night, and it soon became compulsory for our men to man defensive positions during the night. The area was deemed to be particularly vulnerable, being an important railway junction.

I had heard no more from the War Office about joining the Royal Fusiliers, but one day I received a summons to attend for a medical examination at the neighbouring town of Kirkcaldy. I did not know the outcome of this examination, except that the doctor passed the remark that I was very strong. Then came the letter: report within days to the Guards Depot – in Chelsea, London – to join the Scots Guards. There was little time to prepare. I had to leave my job as a teacher, to the tears of the children and the good wishes of the teachers and staff; my friendly colleagues at the school.

My command of the Thornton Platoon, which by now was renamed the Home Guard, was handed over to my Sergeant. A special parade was mustered with full military dignity: the Area Commander was present, and after speeches and a presentation I was piped off the parade ground by a piper from the depot, the Black Watch.

This was a very important event in my life for, although

the first stage of the war of the *blitzkrieg* had ended, it was clear that if Britain was to survive it must secure the defeat of the German Army, which was by now occupying most of Europe except for the British Isles and part of Russia. The future was bleak and wholly unknown, although nobody contemplated the possibility of defeat.

The few days of freedom that remained were spent in visiting my home at Drumnachochit, where I took my girl-friend Ada to meet my relatives and announced our engagement. I dumped my personal effects with my mother for the duration and, on the appointed evening, caught the night train from Waverley station to London.

Chapter Two

It was October, and dawn was breaking as we approached our destination. We looked out at a scene of progressive desolation as we approached the city centre. Buildings were destroyed and presently we could see whole streets in ruin. These scenes brought home to us the real meaning of war and what it meant to the residents of the great cities of the country.

By now I had made friends with a fellow traveller, who turned out to be on the same mission as me. He turned out to be a former guardsman, retired, and was now returning to the colours. He, of course, knew London, so when we alighted at King's Cross Station he led the way to the Underground. His name was Jock Canon which he acknowledged when we passed through Canon Street Station on our way to Sloane Square. Here we alighted and walked round the corner into Chelsea Bridge Road, where the Guards' barracks were sited.

We had some time on our hands so Jock suggested that we should celebrate the end of our civilian freedom in the local hostelry. There were several Chelsea Pensioners seated in there. Jock told me that they would expect us to buy them a drink, which we did, and we settled down to enjoy their stories of campaigns long ago. With a considerable effort, we rose, paid our respects to the veterans, and toddled down the road to our new home, new life and new world.

The sentry on the gate where we reported summoned the

'stick' who escorted us to an office, where we were embodied, by taking the oath of allegiance to the King, and being issued with a service book, uniform and kit. As I stood in the queue waiting to sign on, I realized that all the others were from different parts of Scotland. In front of me was a tall thin chappie: when I asked his name he replied, 'Richard, but they call me Dick.' In those days Guardsmen had to be quite tall and the squad seemed to muster from about 5' 10" to just over the 6' mark.

From the issue of kit we were conducted to our home – the 'barrack-room'. There we met two regular soldiers – Corporal Scott and Trained Soldier Bennet – who, between them, would be responsible for our day to day training, and for turning us into soldiers within the barrack-room. Then there would be others: terrifying men – till you got to know them. The barrack-room was sparsely furnished: a bed for every man, a coke-fired stove in the middle, a table on each side, lockers by the beds and a cupboard attached to the wall above each bed.

We were told to pick ourselves a bed and change into our military garb, the outer part of which in the first place was a denim jacket and trousers. The khaki uniform would not be worn until we had been properly fitted by the tailor. There were two hats – a 'fore and aft' and a 'cheese cutter' – two pairs of boots, socks, tie, two khaki shirts, a pair of mitts, a greatcoat, pullover, handkerchiefs and cap badges. The kit included toilet accessories, cutlery, bayonet, belts, haversacks, blankets and groundsheets, all to be signed for.

Then we went on to the barber, who completed each cut in about a minute. The electric machine rendered the hair very short and only a longer frill or 'dosan' at the front was left to make something of. My moustache was left *in situ* without demur, so it was down to the canteen.

There were hundreds of soldiers in this hall and we took our place at tables reserved, once only, for the 'rookies'. By following the rest to the distribution point, we got our plates full and returned to our tables to consume the offering. Suddenly there was a hush and one was aware of a magnificent Guards officer, accompanied by NCOs, walking round the tables. As he approached a table, all seated there leapt to their feet. A Sergeant Major barked out the words, 'Any complaints?' To raise a complaint one would have to be very sure of himself and the nature of the sub-standard food provided by His Majesty. In the absence of a complaint the party moved on to another table, and so on. If a complaint was registered, the details were taken down and the complainant warned to stand by for further investigation.

Having consumed our ration, we returned to the barrack-room, where the Trained Soldier had us sorting out our kit and making our beds. For our part, we engaged each other in conversation and tried to sort out who our likely friends would be, for we would need friends in this new situation of our lives. We learnt that we would not get outside the barrack gates – or, as the Army has it, 'walk out' – for six weeks, until we could conduct ourselves as soldiers and as Guardsmen.

It was about 8 p.m. that the air raids usually started, and our first night in Chelsea Barracks was no exception. We had seen, on our way in, the damage and destruction to buildings in the vicinity: the crazy sight of blocks of flats, sliced in half with rooms and furniture displayed and no outer wall. First there was the siren, warning people to take cover. We just stayed where we were and listened to the Trained Soldier recounting the history of the Regiment; the number of Field Marshals, Victoria Crosses and Battle Honours which this illustrious regiment had acquired over the years. Next came the throbbing sound of the German bombers, together with illumination from the searchlights, and the thunder of the anti-aircraft guns, or 'ack-ack' as they were popularly known. For the next half hour or so pandemonium reigned, with bombs bursting and guns booming. Suddenly it all slackened off and silence reigned once more. This was the lot of the Londoner for months on end. The population never complained or thought of treating for peace or clemency.

As our training programme developed, we went out of barracks, for cross-country runs and elementary manoeuvres, usually across the river into Battersea Park. The Londoners went about their business stoically, although there was rubble and destruction everywhere. Our route marches were most enjoyable. The officer in charge was reputed to be the brother of the Queen, and when we halted for our ten-minute rest in the hour, he would distribute cigarettes to the men. As the days passed we were slowly being turned into soldiers.

Chelsea Barracks were quite old and Spartan in their provision. The washrooms consisted of a few metal sinks, served by a cold water tap. There was a large mirror running the length of the washbasins. The morning ablutions were a pantomime, for dozens of men crowded round the sinks to shave, with the help of the Army issue shaving stick, brush and safety razor. You looked up, into the mirror, to locate your own face, in a sea of similar faces covered with soap, and hands uplifted to perform the intricate task of removing the offending stubble. Failure to secure a close shave might have one in serious trouble later.

The barrack-room boasted a wireless which, under the control of the Trained Soldier, produced popular music featuring Vera Lynn, the Forces' Sweetheart, crooning such numbers as *The White Cliffs of Dover, Yours till the Stars Lose their Glory,* and other popular numbers of the day.

Our chores included scrubbing and polishing floors, the latter with the help of a 'bumper'. Our boots took hours to bring to a high state of polish, finally achieved by rubbing the leather with the bone handle of a toothbrush. Webbing equipment was treated with khaki Blanco and brasses brought to a high state of shine with the help of the famous 'Brasso' polish. The rifle was our personal weapon at this stage and kept in perfect working order; clean, bright and slightly oiled.

Wartime it may have been, but on the parade ground the ceremonial drill of the Guards was still practised, and every Saturday morning saw a rehearsal of the basic movements of Trooping the Colour. To improve my turn-out and brighten up the appearance of my rifle, I had the woodwork on one side professionally French polished by a little man in Sloane Square, all organized by the training staff. The bayonet scabbard was also lacquered further, ensuring the occasional compliment on parade.

The Saturday morning 'swank' parade was a combined affair comprising the other Guards regiments – the Grenadiers (Bill Browns), the Coldstreams (Lily Whites), the Irish (Micks) and the Welsh (Taffs) – and ourselves, the Jocks. All three bands would be present – military, fife and pipe – sounding off to a chorus of bawling Sergeant Majors, flourishing their pace sticks to ensure that every man's step was of regulation dimensions. One stepped off in slow march, changed to quick march, and from time to time one took a movement of the eyeball to the right or left to ensure that one was in line. The halt was brought about by a mighty double crash (because the Guards' method of halting or turning about is different from any other branch of the service). On the halt, rifle drill was practised, followed by inspections. Finally we would march off to our various areas of barracks, to the tunes of the different regiments of the brigades. In the afternoon, the band would play on, on the drill square, to ensure that good morale was maintained.

There was also sport, compulsory or voluntary. In the former was cross-country running and boxing, in the latter football, rugby and hockey. Running took place in Battersea Park, boxing in the gym. In the latter one of my opponents obtained a discharge owing to a fractured eardrum. I played rugby on Saturday afternoons for the seventh fifteen.

Evenings in the barrack-room were usually organized by the Trained Soldier. This would take the form of squad instruction. It could take any form, depending on the whim of the moment. Practice in giving and shouting verbal instructions was one that satisfied his bird-like brain. If you did not possess a naturally loud voice you could be made to stand on the barrack-room table and shout 'help'. When the Trained Soldier was satisfied that the shout was adequate, the recruit was permitted to resume his place on the barrack-room floor. Another trick of the Trained Soldier was to throw your bedding and inspection equipment out of the window, following the daily inspection round of an officer or sergeant. If the slightest discrepancy was spotted and remarked on, after the inspection, this is what happened, because the criticism would bring discredit on him. We were on the second floor up, so when we discovered that our kit had been jettisoned out the window we had to retrace our steps two floors and then down into the dry moat which fronted the building. A speck of dust on a comb was enough to give rise to such desperate measures.

Fortunately, however, the Trained Soldier had weaknesses, and one of these was shortage of ready cash; life was easier for those who were able to come to his rescue with a bob or two. Money was scarce everywhere. Pay parade was on a Friday and after deductions from the gross weekly wage of 14s., one received about 8s. in one's hand; the financial reward for service to King and Country. Many of the chaps had some sort of payment from their former employment, but I had none. I had been employed as a teacher in Fife, but the county council had decided to make no financial gesture towards their employees in the services, and to my knowledge were the only Local Authority in the country to do so. The staff of the school, however, aware of the plight of their colleagues, would send once a month a parcel containing cigarettes, chocolates and Postal Order, to demonstrate their support for the impoverished soldiery. Such a gesture was greatly appreciated, not only be me but by my friends as well.

At last the great day came when we were allowed to 'walk out'. Our little group of four, after an orgy of spit and polish, passed through the gates of Chelsea Barracks to savour the pleasures of the Metropolis. Of these there were many and varied. The cinema was the premier attraction: Leicester Square, with all its glitter and glamour even in wartime, was a magnet. High tea or similar 'nosh up' would be taken at one of the many clubs for soldiers round the West End. For 1s. 6d. one could get a slap-up meal. The public houses of the West End of London were ever welcoming. They were comfortably appointed and exuded a hospitable atmosphere. We were Guardsmen and we realized that the people of London had a great regard for their Guardsmen. The civilian customers would insist on paying for our drinks and would not hear of reciprocation. We did not feel that this was right but came to accept it in the long run.

The bombing over London continued persistently at this time and, on the principle that what goes up must come down, splinters from our own anti-aircraft shells rained down from on high as well as the German bombs. When out in the open we wore our steel helmets, and from time to time, a small piece of shrapnel would bounce off the helmet. One night we were dancing at a club for Scots servicemen in Park Lane. The band was playing merrily in the window alcove of a very large room. The floor was packed with dancers when, *Bang*, a bomb landed in the garden behind the house and blew out the window where the band was playing. The lights went out and the great chandelier crashed to the floor. Candles were lit: everybody was covered with dust and plaster; some were lying about, dazed. As more light was produced, brooms were brought and the place tidied up. Within half an hour, the band had recovered, returned to the windowless alcove and struck up the music. People dusted themselves, and got back to their dancing, with the light of lots of candles.

We had another near miss when we were returning late one night by Underground. We alighted at Sloane Square station and, as usual, made our way round into Chelsea Bridge Road, when there was a great bang some distance behind us. We rushed for cover at the barracks, but on returning next day we discovered that where the station was, there was now a large hole. But again, before the end of another week the station was open for passengers.

These outings were very pleasant but not all that frequent for, in addition to our normal duties, we had what the army called 'fatigues'. One of these was 'spud bashing', which meant that one had to report to the cookhouse where, with other members of the fatigue, one was presented with a huge mound of potatoes. These you had to peel or scrape and make ready to go into the boiler for the main dinner of the day, which always contained a goodly portion of potatoes. Scrubbing and polishing of floors meant getting down on your knees with a bucket, scrubbing brush and cloth. With your mates, you gradually covered the floor, which in some cases could be enormous – as, for instance, the gymnasium. If the fatigue was a punishment, you could find yourself alone on such a task. On one occasion, I was involved in such a fatigue. My dress consisted of the denim tunic and trousers, neither of which fitted very well; the hair was short like a convict's and on my head was the cap-comforter, a jersey-type headpiece which could be folded into a variety of shapes. An orderly came and said that I was required at the guardroom. I duly accompanied him there, to find my cousin, Kate, who had come to take me out. Kate, by now, was an officer in the Catering Corps of the Women's Auxiliary Force, and by comparison with my state of dereliction, was immaculate. When she saw me with bald head and neck encased in a collar which was made for an Aberdeen Angus bull she wept. I was told to return to our billet, get dressed and that permission to walk out with my cousin had been granted. It was a different looking soldier who joined my cousin at the gate: boots, badges, buttons and belt all shining, ready to walk out on the town and a credit to my regiment. By now, of course, my mates inside had got to know so we set off to a cacophony of wolf whistles from the upstairs windows. The theatre seats and restaurant were of the best, for nothing but that was good enough for Kate. I was duly dropped off at the barrack gate at 11.59 p.m. – the traditional limit imposed by the Army for a walking-out warrant. After that time you are absent without leave: AWOL!

Weeks later I was ordered to parade at the orderly room,

where interviews for commissions were being held. The board consisted of high-ranking officers of the Brigade of Guards, together with two officers of the Canadian Army. I was marched in at high speed and then asked questions which only required single word answers. When I tried to expand, perhaps to point out that I had come from the Highlands of Scotland, the Sergeant Major would shout, 'Stop talking, man'. I had said very little when the Colonel nodded to the Sergeant Major with the words, 'Carry on, Sergeant Major,' who responded with the words, 'Salute the officers. Aboot turn. Quick march,' and in a flash I was out in the corridor again, heading back to my base and a barrage of questions from my mates.

The bombing of London was increasing in intensity and one morning after a particularly heavy raid, the whole of London seemed to be on fire. From time to time we as soldiers assisted in cleaning rubble to help rescue people from underneath. The military authorities probably thought that the time was ripe to evacuate us to the country in the interests of greater safety.

Chapter Three

So it was that, on a Saturday morning before Christmas, we marched out of Chelsea Barracks, behind the band, down Victoria Street, Buckingham Palace Road, past the Palace and eventually into Waterloo Station, where we boarded a train. As we prepared to leave, the band played *Auld Lang Syne* and we all waved to the porters and other rail staff who were standing disinterestedly by.

Our destination, which was of course secret, was West Wickham in Kent, and our new home was Wickham Court Hotel, reputed to have been the home of Anne Boleyn. It had obviously been quite luxurious, for the carpeting and furnishings were of the highest quality. The bedroom furniture had been removed and the soldiers were provided with three boards on two six-inch plinths, with three pads or 'biscuits', to act as beds. The building was ideally situated for the countryside and sported a large car park which was used for drill. The countryside gave scope for greatly extended battle drill and for cross-country runs which took place frequently notwithstanding the weather covering everything in a deep blanket of snow.

There was little in the way of entertainment. There was a pub in West Wickham which was out of bounds on three nights a week, when it was taken over by the Canadians. It wasn't thought to be a good thing to permit the two armies to drink in the same pub. Christmas came and went with little celebration and soon after we were on the move again.

This time it was to the Guards depot at Caterham. This represented a step up in our training, for here everything was on a big scale. We marched from West Wickham to Caterham behind the pipe band, rifles at the slope, and the measured tread to the beat of the drum.

Caterham was a dour place, with low buildings, a high perimeter fence and an enormous parade ground. I got myself a stiff back one night on sentry duty at Fox gate. When my turn to sleep came I lay down on a spring mattress with nothing below, all the blankets and greatcoat above my prone body, for it was a very cold night and snow lay deep on the ground. The frost and cold wind crept up to my unprotected back which on waking up was stiff and rigid. This was a lesson I never forgot.

The great parade ground enabled us to perfect our drill and march discipline. We missed London down there, for Guard duties no longer took us out of barracks to such places as 'Bucks', the Bank or 'Jimmies'. There was one thing we learned and that was to 'shout'. We were lined up on opposite sides of the square and had to drill an opposite number, by shouting the commands across a hundred yards of space. The outcome of all this was that the body was trained to a high pitch of physical fitness by a rigorous regime of training. The mind, on the other hand, was exercised by rehearsing instructions from training manuals and weapon training. Finally our souls were looked after by the Padre, who provided us with one of the few respites from the unending routine of duty, so to a man we would opt to attend the service of the Church of Scotland.

Then came an eventful Saturday morning. I was engaged in a routine scrubbing of the gymnasium floor. The orderly appeared and told me to report, at the double, to the orderly room. There I was marched in before the Adjutant, who read a communication from the War Office that 2700410 Guardsman Grant P had been granted a commission in the QO Cameron Highlanders, as from that day, and would proceed forthwith to join the First Battalion at Beverley in Yorkshire. The Adjutant could hardly believe what he was reading, for facing him was an unkempt looking man, straight from a scrubbing fatigue.

A travel warrant and a ration would be provided and transport would take me to the station in half an hour. I was marched back to the barrack-room where I quickly packed my kit bag and haversack and tried to explain to my friends who had gathered round. They were as non-plussed as I was, so with a wave and 'Best of luck' off I went to join the waiting truck and the journey to the nearest railway station.

I was in full marching order, with full packs, pouches, kit bag, tin helmet, rifle and bayonet. The local train brought me to London, after which I found my way by Underground and then from a mainline station to York and finally to Beverley.

My thoughts were very mixed at this time. I had enjoyed my tenure in the Scots Guards. I had made many friends and we had enjoyed good times together. The hard and testing times we had endured with good humour, and we knew that it was only by these high standards of fitness and expertise that men could properly be expected to enter the field of war. Our training was undoubtedly second to none. I knew the intricate drill movements of the Brigade of Guards, I knew my arms drill and I knew how to maintain and use my infantry weapons, and had won the Empire Medal at the depot for shooting. I knew that from now I would be in a different role. Instead of receiving orders and reacting immediately to them, I would be giving orders and expecting them to be carried out quickly and efficiently. I had the confidence of knowing that my preparation was as good as the best anywhere.

Eventually I arrived at Beverley, where I was received by a sergeant. There was some confusion, for he had been told to expect an officer and here was only a private; so far I had no badges of rank. However, my papers were in order and he accepted the situation as it was. He then explained that the Battalion was no longer in Beverley, having moved the previous day, further into Yorkshire at Thorne. I would therefore remain there for the night with the 'rear detail', and move on in the morning.

Next morning a unit PU with driver turned up from Thorne to collect me and at the same time pick up the Adjutant who had broken his leg and was being discharged from the local hospital. He appeared on crutches and greeted me jovially as one of the boys, although I had not yet acquired a pair of 'pips'. On arrival at Thorne, the snow lay deep on the ground: the country was flat and the canals which seemed numerous were frozen over. I was told that I would be allocated to 'D' or Don Company, as it was known in military circles, and was duly delivered to its billet, which was none other than the local 'work house'.

I was to be 16 Platoon Commander and my fellow colleagues were Allan McKillop – an Invernessian – and Archie Fallow – a laughing, joking banker from Glasgow. The Company Commander was Colin Hunter, who had served with the Fourth Battalion in France, was taken prisoner and had escaped back to his native land. His second-in- command was Bill Dewar. The three Platoon Commanders occupied a room in the work house where the troops of 'D' Company were billeted. The walls of the room were dripping wet, but we sought to counter the effects by maintaining an enormous fire, day and night.

The officers wore the kilt both with battle dress and in the mess, which was sited in a local pub, the Red Bull. To get to the mess one had to walk, so, in order to avoid embarrassment, I was lent a Tam o'Shanter bonnet with Cameron cap badge and a pair of pips, so that I now passed as an officer in battle dress. In the mess all was gaiety and *bon homie*. I met all my brother officers and of course the Commanding Officer, Lt Col Pat Hannay, who invited me to sit by him at dinner. At his request I regaled him with my experiences in the Guards which caused him to laugh heartily.

Although I had no great experience of liquor, I was able to hold my drink with the best of them, on this testing occasion. In the morning I paraded before the CO who greeted me officially, then granted me 48 hours' leave to go up to Edinburgh to get kitted out as an officer in the Camerons. He then bid me good luck and handed me over to the Adjutant for detailed briefing. He, in fact, was leaving the following day and was handing over to Neil Baird. I was given a detailed list of items to purchase, a rail pass, £40 uniform allowance and, to save further expense, I was sold an officer's greatcoat at a knock-down price. Then it was on to the Quartermaster for fitting of battle dress and other accoutrements, Cameron style.

Now it was back to the work house to meet my platoon, which consisted of a sergeant and platoon headquarters; three sections, each commanded by a corporal. As I went along the ranks I talked to each man in turn. It was necessary to get to know them, for from that moment I was their commander, and as the Battalion was deployed for the counter-attack in case of invasion, we might see action at any time.

Next day I departed for Edinburgh, where I visited the

regimental tailors, Willie Anderson of George Street. He literally took me over, and within hours I had a Balmoral and Glengarry fitted with badges, tunic in Barathea, kilt, sporran, Sam Browne belt, hose, and black brogues and a raincoat. I did not require an 'ash plant' walking stick, because I already had one from Glen Urquhart. The ash plant was always carried by the Highland Officer in and out of battle. I changed into the new dress, put my battle dress into a case, met my fiancée and had a meal at the Officers' Club, before catching the train back to Thorne in time to be on parade on Monday morning.

I was soon to realize that a Highland regiment is very much a family unit, of which I was to be a member for the next four or five years. The sound of the pipes was the rousing call of reveille, every morning, to the tune of *Hey Johnnie Cope*. A few minutes later the batman would come in and rouse you with a mug full of tea, or commonly called in the Army a 'mug of char'. From that moment there was little time for prevarication. The routine was jump up, wash, shave, dress in shorts and singlet, socks and boots and out into the snow for half and hour's PT with the men. On one or two mornings, however, the routine was different when we, the officers, indulged in Highland dancing under the direction of the Pipe Major. Then it was back to the billet, dress for the day and up to breakfast in the mess, where the programme for the day would be discussed.

At Thorne the mess was on a Battalion basis and catered for all officers, presided over by the Commanding Officer; an older man, irascible and wearing the ribbons of the First World War. He swore frequently and uttered quaint phrases, with a coarse innuendo, such as when annoyed or frustrated, particularly on the telephone: 'Stuff me with a green banana', 'Balance me on the end of a sticky p——k'.

He was a fair man and quite liked by the rank and file, particularly the 'regulars'.

The First Battalion was of course a regular formation but in order to bring it up to wartime strength, particularly after Dunkirk, it was being infiltrated by conscripts and former territorials. This meant that the senior NCOs were regulars and the privates in the main conscripts, but a few of the latter were beginning to emerge as junior NCOs. It was more or less the same with the officers, for the subalterns were practically all wartime entries to the Army, some of the captains were ex-Territorials and the field rank were regulars.

The mess was in the Red Lion pub at Thorne, which had been requisitioned for the purpose. The only amenity it had was a long oak dining table which came in very useful on formal mess nights, when the full ceremonial of a Highland regiment mess night was observed. The CO sat at the head of the table and at the other end facing him was Mr Vice, usually the senior subaltern. Tartan trews were worn on these occasions, rather than the kilt, but Sam Browne belts were not worn, and would be hung on the hall stand. At the end of the meal when coffee was being served, the carafe of port would appear and, after the CO had poured himself a glass, it would circulate always to the left and never go back a place. At the appointed time the CO would call out 'Mr Vice, the King' and Mr Vice would solemnly stand up, call upon all assembled to do likewise, and propose the toast of the monarch. On certain very special occasions, this was drunk in Highland style by everyone standing on their chair with one foot on the table, when the liquor was consumed, thrusting their glasses over their shoulders.

During the meal, which was served entirely from platters with each diner helping himself, the pipers would play, marching round the table, halting and resting for a reasonable time between blows. After the Royal toast there would be the Subalterns' Four, which was a Highland reel, danced by four chosen subalterns. The dancing expertise was part of the regimental tradition and was practised as part of the physical training programme for the officers. It was of course part of the stock-in-trade of all members of the pipe band; drummers as well as pipers. The Subaltern's Reel was the signal for the start of fun for the evening. With more dancing, singing and a general display of horseplay – taking the form of little contests of strength – the visitors always enjoyed themselves, were made very welcome, and always wished to be asked back again. Visitors included people of very high rank, both in the armed forces and the government, and sometimes even royalty, but in the mess there was a spirit of equality, as well as deference to the guest, which led to a very friendly, if sometimes boisterous, atmosphere.

There were always certain absentees from such occasions – the duty officer. The duty officer would remain in the orderly room all night. He would take his bed with him: consisting of camp bed, holdall – a kind of sleeping bag which was fleece lined and also carried one's blankets – blankets, shaving kit, etc. At times agreed upon with the Adjutant, he would go out and visit the guards sited at various places in the town of Thorne. This was a hazardous duty because it took place at an hour of extreme darkness and the first one knew of the presence of the sentry was to see the point of a bayonet at the throat and hear the challenge, 'Halt! Who goes there?'

'Friend.'

'Advance, friend, and be recognized.' The password was exchanged and when the sentry was satisfied, the officer was given the VIP treatment, and even a cup of tea, before proceeding to the next post.

The winter of 1940–1 was very severe: the snow lay deep for weeks and the canals were frozen. Our room in the work house kept dripping and the batmen were sorely tried keeping the fire going. My batman was now Pte William Mac-Dougal from Inverness, so we were on the same wavelength and he quickly asserted his authority among his peers. He was a little man but sharp, talked very fast and was more or less incoherent to anyone hailing from beyond twenty miles of Inverness. He was never what one might describe as a smart soldier but was a survivor and always able to acquire the basic essentials of life. He required quite a bit of instruction in how to keep his officer in a constant state of smart appearance: boots, shoes, Sam Brownes, badges and buttons had to shine and his fighting gear had to be clean, bright and slightly oiled at all times as well. These batmen had to learn the techniques of serving food in the mess, as and when required.

Route marches of great length, and deployment in the countryside, formed a solid part of our training. There was one occasion when we were all transported to the artillery ranges in the border hills of Northumberland, where we underwent experience of moving up under artillery barrage, with live shells, to a point as near the objective as was safe from bursting shrapnel. This was the basis of the infantry attack, with close support from the guns. When the course was over, we marched back to Thorne; a distance of well over a hundred miles. We spent nights on the road putting up in barns and outhouses and other suitable shelter before moving on in the morning. On two nights there chanced to be dances in the nearby villages, to which some of us went, and where we danced, till three in the morning, in our army boots which had already carried us over 30 miles that day.

In the town itself, and its district, Yorkshire hospitality was soon manifesting itself. People invited us out to their homes and club, and it was even suggested that parents had an eye on us as possible spouses for their daughters! Out in the country on manoeuvres, I would halt my platoon for a rest in a village and it would be no more than a few minutes before the women were out with jugs of tea and pork pies, complete with the traditional egg in the centre. Food fit for the gods, and certainly for the kilted Cameron Highlanders.

But we were not all from Cameron country. I had quite a few Yorkshiremen in my platoon. Finer men you could never meet; good athletes, good soldiers and good men. There was one little problem; coming from Yorkshire they would seek 48 hours' leave to visit their families at the weekend and would find means such as getting onto the platform with a platform ticket and travelling to and fro on this. Stationmasters would complain, but never could catch the culprits. I must admit to having been very disinterested in the problem. By now I had built up a very good rapport with my platoon and felt that if and when the time came we would be able to give a good account of ourselves.

On the personal side I had been moving towards marriage. Ada Alan lived in Edinburgh and was a teacher there. To get married I would have to go there, and leave would be necessary. Two things were required of the Commanding Officer: his permission to get married – which he gave after a few pertinent and searching questions – and leave of absence for the wedding and honeymoon. I said that I had had no leave since joining the Army, which he laughed to scorn, saying that he had had no leave since before the war started. However, in the goodness of his heart, he gave me 48 hours' leave for all purposes, from the Friday night until the Sunday night. I duly made my preparations and on the appointed hour stepped out of the work house to the truck which was to take me to the station; but instead of a truck it was a wheelbarrow, into which I was ceremoniously dumped. The pipe band was in attendance and off we went in the wheelbarrow, behind the pipe band, to the cheers of the raucous soldiery, all the way to the station.

I boarded the train, and arrived in Edinburgh in the early evening, proceeding to the home of a relative where my brother Jim was waiting to do the honours of Best Man on the morrow; which, when it came, saw the necessity for completing some of the details of dress and turn-out necessary for the occasion. There were one or two small matters I wanted to discuss with my future bride and therefore called on her briefly, although this was frowned upon.

My brother and I arrived at the church in good time to have a chat with the guests, until the Bride and Minister were ready. No problems here and we were duly wed in the traditional Scottish style. From the church the bridal party went straight to the photographic studios and then on to the reception at the Royal British Hotel. Relatives and friends had gathered from afar under wartime conditions, which were far from easy. Nonetheless they were a cheerful bunch and made use of all the traditional wedding tricks, even to the rice and confetti shower when we went to board our train for York in the evening.

On arrival at York we booked in at the Station Hotel and were duly shown to our room, which to my horror contained twin beds. I made my position very clear to the bellboy, and in a matter of seconds we were shown into a double-bedded room – much more appropriate for the honeymooning couple. I had to pop downstairs to arrange the menu. There I met an officer of the Royal Scots whom I knew and adjourned to the bar with him, realizing half an hour later that I had left my bride upstairs in the bedroom. However, during the evening he helped me make amends for the lapse.

Sunday morning was lazy and restful then by train back to Thorne and our married lodging – an officers' married quarter with a couple who spoke the strange language of South Yorkshire: 'Oos is gan to 'Atfield ba boos'. But the evening saw my colleagues waiting for us at the local hostelry, and high jinks. The peace of our slumbers was broken in the morning by a bang on the bedroom door, followed by a couple of mugs of tea, as the door opened to reveal Pte William MacDougal, batman, who greeted the bride as a long-kent friend.

Ada, being an army bride, had to meet the other wives and develop some sort of social life with them, while their menfolk were out on their never-ending military manoeuvres.

I had to proceed on army courses such as physical training and unarmed combat, platoon commanding and aircraft recognition, all of which, particularly the first, turned me into a condition of physical fitness that was never matched in peace time. Unarmed combat taught me to look after myself in any situation and not rely altogether on the use of weapons. The Glasgow Billy Boys had nothing on us.

Soon we moved north still in Yorkshire to the pretty town of Knaresborough where again I occupied a married quarter, this time in a large old-style house where one never knew who the other occupants were. Here we were but a company strong, the rest of the Battalion being dispersed over a wide area, including Harrogate. The HQ mess was in the golf clubhouse and free golf was available to the officers at all times. I never knew what happened to the members ousted from their club.

Being on a company footing, and none of the other officers being married, we were able to provide quite a bit of hospitality in this large domain. I drew rations and fed at home. MacDougal was responsible for fetching the basic rations from the company cookhouse and very liberal they were. On one occasion he was seen walking along the main street with a bag containing rations, out of which a string of sausage links hung loosely, except that a dog kept on shortening the links by a sausage every ten steps.

Our role here was the counter-attack. Landings would take place on the coast and would be briefly held by the coastal defence and Home Guard. We would embus, drive like mad through the unsignposted countryside, supported by the heavy stuff, to deliver the counter-blow before the enemy could get time to consolidate their early advantage. It was very easy to get lost in the maze of roads usually at night, halting at dawn in a village, and asking an old boy where we were, to be told that he didn't know. This, of course, was in accordance with the security warnings given out by the Government at the time. All this time we were smothered in Yorkshire hospitality both official and private.

Then one of these orders which come in the army: get ready to go abroad. Tropical clothing was issued, jabs were given, wills were made, and farewells progressively made. It was a time of considerable jollity because the British tropical uniform – consisting of the pith helmet or *topee*, the long jacket or tunic with long pockets, and the extraordinary shorts with turn-ups, which could be turned down to make short longs at night – when worn, produced a comical sight, and as there weren't many sizes one had to adopt a size as approximate as possible.

The public did not, of course, know about these moves but it was strange that a Scots lady living in the Grand Hotel Harrogate put on a special ceilidh and dinner for the Cameron officers and wives and, as she was reputed to be strongly linked with whisky, there was very little hardship endured on that evening. No mention was of course made of the projected departure, which suddenly was called off, and normal duties resumed. Just as well, because we might have gone to Singapore and fallen straight into the hands of the invincible Japanese Army.

Then we moved south to Oxfordshire, to which we marched and rode by stages, stopping at large mansion houses on the way, where the lord of the manor was pleased to do his best for the military, as long as they fed themselves.

Our company, Don, under the command of Colin Hunter MC, was allocated to the village of Deddington, the Battalion HQ being a few miles further on, at Adderbury. Deddington was an old-fashioned village, of Cotswold stone: an open drain ran through the main street and many houses were thatched. Our Company HQ was in a pleasant house on the Oxford road, across which was a manor house, in which dwelt three or more girls, daughters of the Duke of Marlborough; Churchills no less. Ada and I were billeted in a cottage with no bathroom. When baths were required a long tin receptacle was brought out by the landlady and duly filled with hot water from kettles and pans. The batmen liked this place and converged there for coffee with Ada, for which there was considerable reciprocation by way of fodder, firewood and other necessities. Being so far from Battalion HQ gave us considerable freedom of action which was much appreciated. There was a good deal of socializing with the local village hierarchy, and few dull moments.

Colin Hunter, our CO, got married while we were there, to the sister of the Adjutant, Neil Baird, and there were drinks all round. The other officers were Bill Dewar, Allan McKillop and Charles Hayes, and marching through the winding roads of Oxfordshire was the order of the day. Assault landings across the canal were practised and swimming with full kit and boots was an activity practised under strict supervision, and not too frequently, because of the problem of drying the clothing.

It was at this time too that the summons came for me to sing before Queen Mary, the dowager queen at the time. I had established myself as a singer in the mess, so it appears that a signal came from Southern Command for the Battalion to provide a singer of Scottish songs for an entertainment provided for Queen Mary and her household at her wartime residence; Badminton Palace in Gloucestershire, the home of the Duke of Beaufort. It appears that every Thursday afternoon she had an entertainment followed by a film for the benefit of her household.

On the appointed day, a soldier accompanist and I piled into a 15-cwt truck with the Southern Command entertainments officer, and proceeded westwards to Badminton. I had assiduously practised Scottish and Gaelic songs in the backroom of the local pub, and I had prepared a programme, with English translations in the case of the Gaelic songs, to be submitted to Her Majesty. We had to bring our own tea and sugar for the tea which followed, because of the strict rationing at the time – royalty were no exception. Having arrived at the house, we were ushered into the hall where the concert was to be held. This was a magnificent room, entirely of marble, with a grand piano at one end and rows of chairs with a very elaborate gold-decorated one in the middle of the front row. I was dressed in the Cameron officer's uniform, with kilt, and my accompanist wore battledress.

We were provided with programmes, and arranged our music as the audience filed in. They consisted of the guard and workers in the estates, for Queen Mary organized wood chopping sessions every day for all members of her retinue. At a given signal all stood up and in came the stately lady Queen, followed by the Duke and Duchess of Kent and their Graces of Beaufort, two children of the Queen and two children of the Kents. Other important people such as ladies-in-waiting and equerries also took their seats. Her Majesty was handed a very large and pretentious programme, complete with ribbon binding, and at a nod the concert started.

I introduced each item before singing and finished the programme with a pre-arranged request from Her Majesty of a popular song at the time, *There'll be someone waiting there, over the hill*. Gaelic songs, such as *Kishmul's Galley*, the *Eriskay Love Song* and *Tha mi sgith* appeared to be well received. The concert was followed by what seemed to be a free viewing of a film, *Citizen Kane*, which seemed to have too much of a psychological bias for the times we were having and for the audience gathered there.

Tea was served in the drawing-room and we were able to circulate freely with all and sundry. The Queen and other royalty could not have been more gracious. My accompanist, who hailed from the Glasgow Gorbals, behaved most naturally – as if he were in his native Sauchie Hall Street, meeting his cronies.

A long drive brought us back to Deddington and the excited interest of our friends, followed in a few days by a visit to the CO's office at Adderbury to hear him read a message of thanks from Her Majesty and to the commanders of the Battalion, Fifth Brigade, Second Division, for releasing us to perform on that occasion.

Not long after this event the Battalion officers' mess decided to give a Highland Ball at Adderbury House, which was the Battalion headquarters and officers' mess. The gentlefolk of the district were invited, in recognition of the hospitality they had extended to the Battalion during its residence in Oxfordshire. Silver was brought down from Inverness, functional as well as decorative, and the finest foods were prepared, including salmon, trout, venison, partridge, pheasant, grouse, teal, snipe, woodcock, and a full range of sea foods from oysters to lobster were brought from the homeland of the Battalion. The regimental band and orchestra rehearsed waltzes and foxtrots, while the pipe band prepared a feast of music, suitable for the occasion, and the subalterns engaged in an orgy of practising the Highland Reel and Argyle Broadsword.

All officers wore the kilt; wives and lady friends were dolled up to look beautiful, friends helping each other with bits and pieces because it was wartime and communications were difficult. The guests came in a motley of dress: some wore regimentals in blue and red, the 'County' came in their pinks and the Lords Lieutenants in sober evening dress with decorations.

Fun and games were the order of the night and it was not just the reels that brought hoots and screams from the dancers but also the Post Horn Gallop, as a gesture to the visitors. The bar – presided over by Lance Corporal Thompson, formerly of the Danum Hotel, Doncaster – produced exotic drinks to excite even the most sophisticated palates. It was generally agreed that a good time was had by all and an aura of goodwill spread in all directions.

The Army is very good at this sort of thing; our open sports meeting, being another example of efficient organization, whereby the size of the arena is laid down in the book, as are the tents and marquees, tracks, pits and other paraphernalia, with timing of events, judging, recording, and finally presentation of trophies, all done according to the laid-down instructions, whilst the band plays suitable renderings of martial and popular music.

Each individual weighed up these events in the light of their own personal experience: some would say that the ball reminded them of that famous or infamous one at Kirramuir, others more romantic to the Waterloo Eve Ball at Brussels, or the Edinburgh Ball for Prince Charlie, before Prestonpans. It seems that the ball takes place before the battle, rather than after. But events were moving fast. Tropical kit was again coming out and soon we were being inoculated for a move overseas. One group of a dozen men were inoculated with petrol by mistake, causing great distress and pain. The medical orderly had put petrol in an empty phial unknown to the doctor, who unfortunately had to take the rap for the lapse.

Then the whole Battalion went on parade at Adderbury for a visit from the monarch himself, King George VI, and it was my honour and duty later in the mess to offer him a glass of whisky, on a silver tray, which he gladly accepted, for it was a cold day. A week or two later, the whole Second Division converged at a spot in the countryside to be inspected by the Premier, Winston Churchill, who was accompanied by his daughter, who raised a great cheer. He then gathered the troops round him and addressed them, saying he would follow their deeds of valour with pride. He left showing a V sign and puffing at a large cigar.

We were given 48 hours' leave, which I used to go home

to Drumnadrochit, to say farewell to my relatives. I arrived about 10 o'clock in the morning and had to leave at 4 o'clock in the afternoon so there wasn't much time for tears or laughter. My grandfather was in his eighties so the chances of seeing him again were slim, but he stood erect and proud as he said goodbye. The others were the same for we all knew that the survival rate of a Highland officer, or for that matter any infantry officer, wasn't very high.

So I left the small group standing there waving and returned to Deddington. Then on a certain night we were told to be ready and told we would be leaving at midnight. Having heard of our departure, all the pubs in the village opened their doors and hospitality, free to the soldiers for the evening, until 11 o'clock, when they had to report for departure. They had come to like the Camerons and many firm friendships had been made. I returned home to Ada and, like all the other married couples, spent the evening hours together until it was time to go.

When I returned to the village square in the dark, I found my platoon sergeant who reported that the men were ready to form up in full marching order, with kitbags, ready to embus into the waiting army lorries. I gave the order to get on parade in three ranks which they did in pitch darkness, but even in the gloom I thought there was something amiss. They didn't appear to stand erect, heads were drooping, rifles fell on the ground, and then I heard the unmistakeable sound of water streaming down on the cobbles. I then realized that they were all very drunk and the streams of water were streams of urine.

The sergeant had of course to agree with me and we had to make the best of the situation. We counted them and found them correct, but not coherent. My magnificent platoon – which had led in games, fieldwork, on the ranges and in drill and smart turn-out – was drunk and incapable, so when it was time to load, Sergeant Campbell and myself loaded them on like sacks of potatoes and off we went to the station where the same operation was carried out in transferring them on to the train. I discovered then that the whole battalion of 600 men was more or less in the same state.

Chapter Four

Off we went, and the rumour got around that it was to Liverpool, for when dawn came we found the train moving through a city of devastation, while our prostrate men in corridors and compartments were slowly stirring, and asking each other what had happened and where they were. Soon we came to a grinding halt, as steam trains did, in the docks, close to a huge liner which seemed to be waiting to take us aboard. We detrained onto the dockside, and the transformation was remarkable: everybody was bright and breezy, sniffing the sea air, laughing and joking. I gave my men a good haranguing and brought them to attention half a dozen times and told them not to let it happen again.

In the mean time the ship's crew started throwing us bars of chocolate. This was something we hadn't seen for years and was much appreciated, although there was far too much of it which had deteriorated from the effect of salt water. In spite of all this the lads ate the chocolate, avariciously, before going on board which was quite soon.

The ship was Dutch, and had been used on the Dutch East Indies run. The *Marnix Van St Aldegonde*, as she was called, was a luxury liner manned by a Dutch crew of Netherlanders, and Lascars from the East Indies, with a good smattering of Chinese. The men's quarters were below and hammocks were provided for sleeping. The officers were three to four in a cabin, placed as strategically near the men as possible.

There were surprises, for soon orders were issued following the requirements of the Captain. The officers would dress for dinner and wear ties at tea and lunch. The dining-room remained in its luxury style as did the menus and standard of serving the food. Drink at table and in the bars was cheap, with whisky and gin selling at 2*d*. a nip, bottles of wine at 2*s*. and brandies and liqueurs at 2*d*. to 3*d*. a measure. Before sitting down to dinner we stood for the Dutch National Anthem, which was a very long one, but we soon realized that we were under the discipline of a martinet and only best behaviour would be tolerated.

As we moved away from the quay we knew not where we were going and soon night removed any idea as to where we were. In the morning, though, we were out in the open sea with nothing but ships around us in lines moving in the same direction with battleships on both flanks. But there was plenty to do. We were introduced to the routine of the sea: lifeboat drill, security and man management in an enclosed space. The training programme had to be devised and put into operation so that the troops could be kept busy, healthy and happy from morning to night. Lectures were frequent as were cinema shows; PE and games on deck helped to take care of spare energy; and there was a small pool aft which was the scene of an enormous amount of horseplay.

We were not alone, for when we got out into the open waters of the North Atlantic, we realized that we were in an enormous convoy: hundreds of ships of all sizes sailing ahead in two lines, with naval escort on both flanks. These naval ships included a battleship and two or three cruisers and innumerable destroyers and frigates. No doubt, down below were submarines prowling after their prey. We were aware that we were steaming in a north-westerly direction and soon the cold weather got colder and the seas rougher.

One night a concert was arranged on deck. I was asked to sing and duly took my place on the stage and roared out the words of *Annie Lawrie* only to find that the wind caught them before they had gone six inches from my mouth; the audience had to use its imagination as to what was being sung by lipreading and following my gesticulations.

Every night in the officers' dining-room we stood for the Dutch National Anthem but a night of nights came when we were invited to celebrate the birthday of the Queen of the Netherlands, Wilhemina. Everything was on the house, including the Bols gin. Most of the officers were very young and not really accustomed to large quantities of spirits, Dutch or Scots, and the result was that quite a lot of damage, mainly I suppose in trying to gain the elevated heights of the top bunks. Our cabin door was completely removed, because the occupiers of the adjacent cabin reckoned that ours was theirs! Apologies were plentiful next day and soon normal relations were established with the Dutch officers and crew.

A daily newspaper was published and talks were given by the officers and any other who could hold the floor for twenty minutes or half an hour. One of the most celebrated was a young padre, for he dealt with the subject of sex and how to keep the urge at a low level when away from one's loved ones. The answer was sublimation, a word quite unknown to the Jocks, but it took the form of writing down all the sexy notions of the marital relations, as credibly, realistically and naturally in the letter home to the wife. On active service all letters have to be censored and for a few weeks the officers were entertained to seething hot descriptions of love-making, real or imaginary, which the soldiers had experienced. I never really knew whether it had the desired effect or not.

I had brought with me a box of paperback books for the edification and pleasure of my men. These I issued one day and by the end of a couple of days they had all disappeared; through the portholes no doubt. There was little interest in culture or learning at that time among the footsoldiers of the British Army.

As the days advanced the weather got colder and the seas rougher – obviously the great armada was thrusting its way through Arctic waters in a westerly direction. Our whereabouts were never discussed nor any information concerning them passed down, but with an intelligent look at the sun's position in the daytime – and the North Star and Plough at night – it was possible at least to make guesses. After a week or two we were aware that we were sailing in a southerly direction. Had we crossed the North Atlantic? We were now sailing parallel with the Canadian and American coasts. The weather was improving and the ships could be seen in their four lines ahead, the battleships keeping their tireless vigil.

Soon the word went round – the Sargasso Sea – for all around us, on the surface of the water, were weeds floating, in some places quite thick. Now we were sailing east: porpoises tumbled about the sides of the ship but kept pace, and the flying fish took off from the ocean and crossed our decks. All these things added to the speculation, for we were now in the tropics and for the first time donned the regulation tropical kit: shirts and shorts in the daytime; the latter having long turn-ups which could be lowered at night to cover the knee in order, we were told, to protect us from the malaria-carrying mosquito. For night the officers replaced the Barathea tunic with a khaki drill jacket cut away at the front for the kilt or tartan trews. To protect us from the heat of the sun we were each the proud owners of the regulation pith helmet.

Land was sighted: 'Where are we?' was the question as the convoy slowed down on entering an estuary. Soon we could see the palm trees on shore and what looked like a small town. It was Freetown, the capital of Sierra Leone. The ships came to a halt in the sheltered waters and there was great speculation about getting ashore. Our ships were surrounded by tenders bearing fresh supplies and by native 'bum boats' selling fruit and leather goods as well as clothing and jewellery. The bargaining was done by shouting, the goods were placed in a basket and hauled up by a rope, then the money was placed in the basket and lowered to the trader who, although his face was jet black, was the proud owner of a name like McKenzie. There was a lot of abuse as well as laughter and I am sure trickery and cheating but generally everyone seemed to be pleased and after a few days we were on our way, this time with a greatly reduced naval escort.

We were now moving in a southerly direction, for one night, in the purple blue of the sky, there appeared the Southern Cross in all its majesty and magic: we were now in the Southern Hemisphere, and soon we were sailing into the most beautiful scene imaginable – Cape Town with the Table Mountain high above, in a matchless backcloth. The troopships, their decks lined with thousands of expectant faces, edged their way into the docks and tied up. Orders were given and rules and regulations issued about our disembarkation, which was to be on the following morning. In the mean time hundreds of South Africans came down to the docks to greet the troops who, though not permitted ashore, were happy to receive fruit of all sorts, chocolates and cigarettes thrown up onto the decks from the dockside.

On the morrow we walked, a bit unsteadily, down the gangplanks onto the jetty, where we formed up by companies after the pipe band, to march to our camp, which was in the race course just outside the city. The roads were lined with cheering people, black as well as white, although occasionally there were people who turned their backs: they were the Boers or Afrikaners who were really supporters of Germany, although South Africa was officially at war with Germany and had a Division in the desert fighting beside the Eighth Army.

We had been told how to behave: not to pick quarrels with the Boers and not to go into District Six which was the preserve of the black people. Visiting cards were shoved into our hands with invitations to visit homes as we made our way to the camp. It was very hot and we realized that conditions in hot countries would be very different to those prevailing at home. The arrangements in the tented camp were excellent, and after lunch we were let out on the town.

I had relations in Cape Town; my mother's cousins lived in different parts of the country, having come with their parents from Scotland in about 1902 to farm in this land of promise. I got on the phone and quickly made my way out to Kalk Bay, accompanied by my friend Willie McKillop, to visit Cousin Elizabeth and her family. They were meeting us at the station and gave us a warm welcome. They looked so like my mother's people, the mother and three children; two girls and a boy. There was no father, however, for Dauncie was up in the desert, fighting with the Cape Town Scottish for the second time in his life, having served in the First World War. However, we were regaled with food and drink and in due course went to another cousin for the remainder of the evening. They lived in an airy bungalow surrounded with palm trees and tropical gardens, and although they still spoke the Scots tongue they appeared to be quite opulent. The other relatives were up country in the

Orange Free State, in the old home near Bloemfontein and in Johannesburg. They entertained us right well but others wanted to extend hospitality to us as well and all in all we had a great time and did very little if any soldiering except for a march through the city to the castle, to show the flag.

On the Saturday night officers were invited to a grand party at the Blue Lagoon Night Club for dinner, drinks and dancing – all of which was fabulous, but the Cape Brandy took its toll and although we were taken to a roadside hamburger stall , where the food was served on shelves clipped onto the side of the car, we had to be helped into our tents and onto our camp beds by our hosts.

In the morning everybody was on parade by platoons. We, the officers, would march our platoons independently out of camp and up to the top of the mountain and return likewise in good order. It should be noted that the men were in no fitter condition than the officers for they had been the recipients of South African hospitality and some had even had a great time down District Six.

At the given signal we moved off and after about two miles of marching, 16 Platoon came to a small native village surrounded by palms and thicket. This is typical all over the countries of the African and Asian continents. I gave the order to halt and fall out for the usual statutory Army rest on a route march. As we sat down, or lay down, on the shady banks just outside the village, out came the natives from their huts, with baskets of fruit on their heads, laughing and dancing about. There were oranges, grapes, bananas, guavas and fruits we had never seen before. We tore into this feast of refreshing fruits and forgot all about our march to the top of the mountain, and then fell asleep for a time. We awoke in consternation that we should now be returning to camp, which we did, and as we passed through the gate there was the General, taking the salute as the platoons passed by. On falling out, I was ordered to return to the General who, to my consternation, complimented me on the turn-out and excellent marching order of my platoon. I saluted with a 'Thank you, Sir', turned about and walked smartly back to my platoon, to give them the good news and told them to keep the episode of the fruit quiet.

On the Monday morning the Battalion marched through the city to show the flag, with the pipe band and everybody wearing the kilt and shirt-sleeve order. After lunch at the castle we went out on the town, to return to camp in a horse-drawn cab, with fruit filling the floor. I insisted on taking the reins, but it was raining and the wheels skidded on the tramcar rails, the cab tilted over: we were all thrown out, including the black cabby, and the fruit was scattered all over the street. It was a moment of indignity, but we got the cab and horse upright, collected the fruit and let the cabby drive us back to camp.

Soon we were preparing to re-embark and it was with a tearful farewell that we took our leave of relatives and friends who had shown us such sumptuous hospitality and demonstrated their loyalty to their British roots.

We slipped out of Capetown quietly in the night, and soon the *Marnix* and other ships of the convoy were steaming into Durban harbour. Here, on the end of the pier, was the 'Lady in White'. She was a woman who greeted all troopships entering Durban harbour by dressing all in white, and singing over a mike and system of loudhailers popular songs of the day and of the Great War, like *Keep the Home Fires Burning, Tipperary*, and so on. Nobody seemed to know her identity but the troops reacted with great gusto and appreciation.

We were now in the war zone and the rumours were

rife. Was it Alexandria and the desert with Monty? Was it Burma where the Japanese were threatening? As we sailed up the coast of Africa we heard that an independent Brigade had been detached from the convoy and had landed on the island of Madagascar, to engage French forces who were in occupation and were in the enemy camp. We also heard that one of our ships carrying vehicles had been sunk by a submarine in the passage between Africa and Madagascar.

Soon we were off Zanzibar and limited shore leave was permitted at Dar es Salaam. This was our first experience of the East, with bazaars, beggars, lepers and the sight of a man with elephantiasis wheeling his own bloated testicles in a barrow. But we still didn't know where we were bound. Back on the ship and away, the direction was east: it was India and straight away preparations were being made for landing at Bombay. The old hands who had been in India before the war gave lessons in Urdu. *Rasta ko Delhi hum ko deklow*: show me the road to Delhi. We were told the soldiers' lore of India in lectures: how the *loose wallahs* would smear their bodies in grease, creep into your tent or railway carriage and steal your rifles, watches and binoculars; how the Indian sun would give you the 'tap' unless you covered your head and spine; and how to avoid drinking water from wells, rivers and lakes, unless properly treated.

The nights in the Indian Ocean were fabulous with fire flies, flying fish, porpoises and always the purple blue of the star-studded sky. But, even at sea, there was the risk of the malaria-carrying mosquito at night and precautions had to be observed by covering as much of the body as possible; not always conducive to comfort in those climates.

Bombay now seemed our definite goal and the Japanese Imperial Army our eventual quarry. So it was that within a few days we were lying off Bombay and preparing to disembark. We were told that on entering port we would remain for two nights on board and then proceed, possibly by train, to a camp. During our stay in the dock area of Bombay we would be permitted to walk out on the city. As I said, from leaving Mombassa we had been well briefed in the ways of India: the monetary system, the bargaining system in the bazaars and a host of other practises which one would have to observe in this the brightest gem in the Imperial crown. India, the home of princes, maharajas, rajas, nizams and lesser potentates, a country with a strict caste system of which we had no knowledge, but about which we would do well to learn.

As is usual on these occasions, three or four friends would agree to go out together and explore the city, which is what we did. The first thing was to hire a cab and ask the cabby to show us the sights. Although English was widely used in India we soon realized that a working knowledge of Urdu was necessary. But a bargain was struck for the hire of the cab for three or four hours, during which time we would see everything. The cabby was as good as his word, taking us to the Gateway of India and along the promenade to the railway station to see hundreds of people squatting and sleeping, waiting perhaps a week for a train. Up Malabar Hill for the views and the towers of silence where the parsees dispose of their dead, to Grant Road, the brothel area, where the women ply their trade in cages, to the finest hotel in Bombay, the Taj Mahal, where drinks are cool and an orchestra plays in the palm court. To the museum and the great shop of the rich, the *Army and Navy*, and so, in the end, we paid him off and thought it a bargain and adjourned to one of the hotels to sample the liquor and food.

We were dressed in accordance with regulations on the

assumption that we would not be returning to the ship until after dark, for darkness falls in the tropics at six. We wore pith helmets, KD shirts and ties, tropical tunics cut away at the front for the kilt, tartan trews, shoes and walking sticks, or ash plants as they were commonly called. At this early stage we still wore the Sam Browne for walking out.

After a sumptuous meal we discovered that there was a dance on in the hotel, later in the evening. We duly got ourselves in, secured a table and prepared for an hour or two treading the light fantastic before returning to the boat. But no, we were to be disillusioned, for although there were lots of women there none of them were prepared to dance with us because we didn't know them – nor were our names on their dance cards. Being a well-disciplined lot we said little, sat around drinking and resolved that the old order of British India would have to change, and change quickly. So eventually we upped and went off back to our home for the past three months; the MV *Marnix Van St Aldegonde*, to rest before the great adventure.

Chapter Five

We disembarked in the morning having said a fond farewell to our hosts: the Dutch Captain and ship's company who had looked after us so efficiently and courteously for the past three months. Every aspect of the journey was in line with the great tradition of the Dutch Mercantile Marine. We grieved to hear several months later that the *Marnix* was sunk by enemy action in the Mediterranean.

The Battalion formed up on the quayside to march to the station. The order of march was the usual one: pipe band, HQ Company, ABC and D Companies in that order. We would march off by companies when the OC saw that there was a reasonable distance between him and rear of the company in front. We in D Company were of course last. Colin Hunter was the OC of Don Company and in due course poised himself to give the order, 'Don Company by the right, quick march' , but he suffered from a stammer and it was only after the fourth attempt that he got past 'Don Company . . .' In the mean time the rear of C Company had disappeared round a corner. Nevertheless we marched off, but did not appear to catch a sight of C Company. Out into the streets of Bombay we went – narrow they were, dirty, sleazy and full of dirty washing hanging overhead – but we were always alone; no sign of the other four companies and the Pipe Band. Colin marched stoically ahead, the little Indian boys ran alongside calling 'Backs heesh' and the dogs barked. He called the officers up and expressed his concern about our whereabouts, but we had no alternative but to march on. We were the British Army in India and could in no way be lost.

At last the van of the company came to an intersection with a main road. The command 'Halt' was given and the officers again called up to see – to our horror, astonishment and relief – the pipe band approaching some distance away down this main street of Bombay. We had obviously taken a short cut and emerged well ahead of the main force. The order to stand at ease was given and as the pipe band – followed by the Commanding Officer, Lt Col Hickson – came up, Don Company was brought to attention. Colin saluted the CO who looked at him in astonishment, as did the whole of the Battalion as they passed, until the last man of C Company passed, when we moved off, wheeled to the left and took up the rear of the force on its way to the station where a train was waiting to transport us.

The Indian train is an extraordinary vehicle, with a variety of carriages, much wider than its British counterpart. The first-class carriages were very sophisticated – with comfortable seating, three-ply windows, loos and showers – whereas the second and third classes were more austere.

All the baggage was stowed away on the train and our personal luggage got into the compartment where we would travel, and so, with cheers to everybody in general, we moved off. As we got under way, after a series of conferences, we were told that we were making for Pashaan camp in Poona: Poona was the fabled home of the 'Sahibs', high on the Deccan plain above Bombay.

There were stops for refreshment and the sales boys crowded round with their wares: leather pocket books – worked in Indian design – cigarette cases, handkerchiefs and so on.

We may have heard of the monsoon at school but really did not appreciate how it operated. It starts to rain sporadically about the middle of June and gathers momentum until sometimes it rains for whole days, pouring down relentlessly then lets up for a day or two, until the thunder and lightning take over again. After about three months it runs itself out.

We marched through Poona to Pashaan camp which was about four miles out of the town, which was very pleasant looking, with its bungalows situated in flowery gardens with bushes and palms in profusion. There did not appear to be the same squalor here as at Bombay.

Eventually we reached the camp with its tents in rows, waiting to house the troops. But instead of being hardstanding, the tents were standing none too securely on a sea of mud. It was mud everywhere: do what we could, it would not go away. To make matters worse, there was little to eat: bananas and tea became the staple diet. It appears that the Indian Army Quartermaster General had forgotten about the arrival of a British Division, with its 20,000 men. But no matter, we had to make the best of it and, above all, prepare for action against the Japanese within a week or so.

Morning runs to the top of the local hill gave us a taste of fitness. The Governor of Bombay Province had his summer residence – in which he and his wife, Lady Lumley, and their children – lived nearby. They invited us in rotation to tea and baths at the Residency, all very sophisticated and pleasant, and before long invitations from the British residents were coming in: as we were a Scots Regiment, there were specific invitations from the Scots residents. There was also a Scots kirk, and the club and racecourse were available to promote social intercourse.

My first foray on the Sunday afternoon was to tea with

a family with Glen Urquhart connections. I hailed a gharry and told him where I wanted to go in Poona. I did not realize the driver was drunk, and before we had gone 50 yards the whole turn-out – horse, gharry, *gharry whalla* and me – landed in the ditch. I pulled myself together, dusted myself down and stood at the roadside to take the situation in, when along came one of our DRs (despatch riders) on a motorbike. He stopped. He was an old soldier and knew the ropes, so he gave the *gharry whalla* a rough time and off we went with me on the pillion, to be dropped off at the bungalow.

The people were very nice but their connection with the home country pretty tenuous and I realized that there was a wide gulf between the natives and the Indian sahibs who had been born and bred in the country. But this was an experience we had to learn: how the sahibs lived, surrounded by servants who did everything for their masters according to their state and rank and were happy in the doing of it.

As one settled down to the country, one realized that, although it was the East, strange languages, customs and religions all were living amicably together in a quiet, sedate manner and, whereas the native read the Indian language newspaper, the British took the *Times* of India which was a near replica of the London *Times*. Likewise the radio: All India Radio catered for English language listeners as well as for the Indian tongues, for – if the truth were known – English was the common language of the whole of the sub-continent.

We were now on a war footing and had to train. The soldier in India had to fight in the North-West Frontier so we were introduced to the training for that sort of warfare. Zarebas were built in the form of stone circles on the tops of hills. These were little forts which were occupied while the main body of troops moved through the valley: the troops occupying the Zarebas would give the necessary protection against the marauding and sharp-shooting Pathaans. To reach these you ran up the hill (*khud*) side, and occupied the little stone circle and when the necessity was passed you vacated same and rushed down to join the rear, hoping that you would not receive a Pathaan bullet in the tender portion of your anatomy in the process.

Conditions in Pashaan camp were quite inadequate for a large concentration of troops, particularly in the monsoon, and although the diet progressed from bananas to something a bit more sustaining, there was always a health risk and this would be fatal to an army about to go into action. Not long after, however, we were on our way to permanent barracks in Secunderabad: a garrison town adjacent to Hyderabad, the Deccan home of the Nizam, considered to be the richest man in the world.

Here was luxury indeed. The buildings were of stone and the roads were tarmacked while everywhere was green grass carefully manicured by the groundsmen. The officers lived in bungalows in gardens kept by the *mali* or gardener, and although you might meet a cobra on the garden path, this was luxury indeed. The officers' mess was large and airy, staffed by Indian servants in magnificent uniforms, performing duties according to their station. Here we learned to address the staff in Urdu: '*Qua hai*,' to the *kitmayar* or waiter, '*hamara wasti do burra pegs, jaldi*,' and in a flash two large whiskies appeared as if from the air. In the kitchens, the *bobajees* prepared meals that were a source of amazement to even the most sophisticated, and the curries on Sundays were out of this world.

The routine on a Sunday consisted of a full Battalion

parade in the morning, with inspection and march past, followed by church. The latter took the form of dividing into the various denominations of Presbyterian, C of E, and RC. By far the largest number were Presbyterian and for this purpose our Battalion Padre was a Church of Scotland minister, Frank McLaughlan. So far as the officers were concerned they had to take turn of commanding the troops, attending the other denominations, and whether it was that Frankie was our own Padre, the behaviour of the troops at his services was much more respectful than that at the others.

Our military and devotional duties having been fulfilled we would adjourn to the mess, where with gins and tonics, or bitters, was the order of the day; a suitable preparation for the curry which was to follow. Back then to the *charpoy* (bed) for a couple of hours then games or sports, taking the form of cricket, hockey, football or running.

It so happened that the Nizam of Hyderabad had an army which had a magnificent cavalry echelon which was not required. The horses and their *seyces* (grooms) he put at the disposal of the officers and it was a treat to get out on the plains on one of these lovely horses (mine was seventeen hands) and spend an hour in the saddle. Some of us were very ordinary horsemen, although I had been acquainted with horses all my life, but others were first class: to wit Angus Douglas, 21/C of the Battalion, a regular who had spent many years in India. On the other hand, Willie McKillop had spent a few years in Central America and loved galloping his steed but got into serious trouble with the CO, Col Hickson, for galloping down the tarmac. Our two Australian officers rode bareback, much to the annoyance of the hierarchy.

Being based in a permanent barracks with ideal conditions we were soon able to absorb the way of life of India:

the climate, and the habits, religion and customs of the people. Although politically, through Gandhi and Nehru, there was some friction with Britain, the people of India loved the British and thought that Queen Victoria was a 'very fine man'.

At hand there were *dursis* (tailors), *munchi* (shoemakers), *dhobis* (washermen) and any other specialist you wish to mention, including the *char wallah* (tea maker), to attend to your needs.

Training was for fitness and on one occasion we marched 50 miles in 24 hours, complete with full kit. We had a Battalion shooting competition for the Mahdi shield, for which I was the runner-up. All these things were contributing to our projected performance on the 'day'. One of our recreational delights was the club at Secunderabad, associated with the swimming pool in the Residents' garden and the golf course, which of course was part of the club amenities.

Then suddenly there broke out civic violence: not against the British but Hindu against Moslem. Killings were rife and the military had to go to the aid of the civil power. Our Battalion was ordered down to Madras state and set up a HQ at Bezwada. Units of platoon size were sent out to trouble-spots and I was despatched with my 16 Platoon to the town of Ellore, about 80 miles away. There I set up a tented camp on the maidan and proceeded to take stock; first of all liaising with the Chief of Police. This was an important town of some 50,000 people and there had been violent rioting. I immediately set about showing the flag by patrolling in strength through the town, leaving a few men behind to guard the camp and prepare the food.

We were called to confront a rioting mob: a rare experience for a greenhorn but we had been told what to do. The police were armed with *latties* (staves) and formed up in three ranks. I formed up my troops in two ranks behind and with a rattle of musketry loaded a round up the spout and applied the safety catch. I stood beside the magistrate who had to give me written authority to fire on the mob, who in turn were shouting, gesticulating and throwing sticks and stones, which fell short. The police were told to advance with their *latties* flailing into the crowd. The front rank broke right and left, and in came the second, doing the same and giving way to the third while the first took over again, and so on. Although the mob stood its ground for a time, they suddenly gave way and bolted.

On our way back to camp we were accosted by a crowd chanting '*Gandhi gu de*' and adopting not so much a threatening attitude but a challenging one of 'find yourselves another way'. I halted the platoon and gave the order to advance in open order with rifles at the port and go in with the boot. This we did and for five minutes a good time was had – on both sides – the mob dispersed, and we reformed and went on our way. This little action became known and we were fêted by the mayor and local big wigs, and supplied with sweet cakes by the local bakers and fruit by the fruiterers.

On the Sunday the local vicar, an Indian of the Church of South India, arranged a church parade for us. All the other Christian missionaries from the Church Army, Salvation Army and a few others were invited to come along. Rifles were piled in the vestibule under guard and all were seated and rose when the procession of clerics came in. The Vicar was in full canonicals but all he had on his feet was a pair of white army socks; no shoes or *chaplis* (sandals). He would normally be bare-footed but this was a fine gesture to the big occasion. He went through the whole service, culminating in a communion lasting an hour and a half. I think the Jocks had had enough.

However, in the evening I had arranged an entertainment of Indian dancers, magicians, strong men and women, jugglers, and magicians, which was an absolute sell out. We didn't have the rope trick, but we did have the boy put in the hamper, tied up, covered with a sheet, with us sitting in a circle around. 'Abracadabra' and the sheets and ropes were removed, the basket lid opened but there was no boy! We clapped, and in he came from behind the onlookers.

The rains came and we had to move our camp to higher ground. Our only communication with HQ was twice a day by wireless. The message came at six o'clock that there was violence at Tarlerpalligudem, which was about 50 miles further on. We were to proceed there and deal with the matter on the spot. Our only transport was a large truck, which was capable of carrying about two dozen soldiers. We had a meal, took supplies on board and turned out in full marching order with the proper issue of ammunition. I sat beside the driver and the Bren gunner in the cab, and my batman, MacDougal, took post over the cabin. We moved off just after midnight, leaving a small rear detail to look after the camp. We travelled slowly through wooded country on a typical dirt track, when suddenly we came to a halt with a tree lying across the road. I got out to investigate but MacDougal shouted, 'Don't touch it, it may be booby trapped!' – he called it boogie trapped. So we reversed the vehicle, disembarked, walked round and made a track for the lorry and so proceeded on our way, with no further incident.

Dawn was beginning to appear in the sky as we neared our objective, and as we approached we could see the glare of fire and hear shots. We were now at the outskirts of the town, or large village, and could see that there was quite a conflagration at a central point which we reckoned to be the police barracks. We assumed that the police station or barracks was being attacked by rioters and so we decided to approach on foot in a state of readiness. Moving off, with rifles at the ready, each man in turn fired a round in the air as we advanced, with the Bren gun on the vehicle coming up behind, covering our advance. Soon we could see figures running away into the morning mist and in a few minutes we were at the barrack gates where a scene of devastation met us.

The rioters had set fire to the buildings: the police had defended themselves with the weapons at their disposal but the rioters, where they could, had thrown police and their wives on the fires. Rifles lay around, with their barrels bent into knots. Seven of the ten police had survived and were able to defend themselves, although very much shaken. There was also an elementary prison block cell, holding about a dozen prisoners, who had not been harmed. Telephone lines had been cut, so we had to use our wireless link back to Ellore and then on to HQ to report the situation.

The situation was now quiet and we prepared a good breakfast and offered the police and their womenfolk, and even the prisoners, tea which was gratefully received, and by noon the police reinforcements arrived and we were able to return to camp, having fired our first shots in anger, although not at a target.

The platoon had acquitted itself well and all the lads were pleased with themselves. On the following night after our return, Sergeant Campbell and I were invited out to dinner at the house of the Church Army Sisters, missionaries, in the town of Ellore. All went well until I spotted Sergeant Campbell making to sip the contents of the finger bowl, notwithstanding the rose petals floating on the top of the water. I stuck my fingers in my bowl, and he got the message in time. The meal was delightful, and the evening was a pleasant break from the routine of camp life.

On Friday night we had orders to return to HQ on the Saturday and while the lorry was manoeuvring, on the Saturday morning, the rear wheels became embedded in the lawn which proved to be a quagmire. All our efforts to get her out failed but, fortunately, another similar vehicle came along, and with its help – plus the platoon, plus half the local inhabitants – we got her on the road, and back we went to Don Company to swap yarns and brag about our exploits.

Next day we returned to Secunderabad by train, the vehicles travelling by road and bringing the equipment. A fascinating thing about rail travel in India was that you stopped at a station for food and drink where everybody was catered for according to their requirements.

We still wore the pith helmet, shirt and shorts, but things were changing: the pith helmet was being discarded for the Scottish Tam o'Shanter and when off duty the shirt was being discarded and 'bare buff' became the order of the day. No harm came although the British Army had worn this type of gear for 200 years, plus spine pads. We didn't get the 'tap' and so old habits were rapidly changing, and a new type of British soldier in India was rapidly emerging.

The training programme was resumed and was directed at assault landings from the sea, fighting in close jungle country and in the open desert type of terrain in extremes of heat and cold. We were now back in Secunderabad and it was late September 1942 when I was called up before the CO and told that I had been selected to proceed on a signal course for officers at Poona, lasting two months.

Off I went and settled in at the Indian Army Signal School, with colleagues from every regiment of the British and Indian Armies. It was a great experience to meet and swap yarns with officers of other regiments; Indian as well as British. We had a room each, with an Indian servant to look after our domestic arrangements, and we ate in the mess where there was also a bar and billiard table. There were parties in the mess and we had the run of different clubs in Poona. The Race Club, on the racecourse, was the scene of dances every Saturday night, and one night I was astonished to see an officer of a Scots regiment dancing on a table, and, looking closer, I recognized him as one who had served in the Scots Guards with me. Another night I visited a Sergeant's mess where a fellow Glen Urquhart man, a sergeant also on a course, Pat McLeod, entertained me right royally in the Sergeants' Mess where he sang *My Granny's Hielan Home*, while I played his accompaniment on an old piano. Finally he organized an escort for me back to my billet.

On the Sunday I would attend the Scots kirk to hear the Reverend Primrose preach, just like home, and invitations to homes were frequent. One was an indirect invitation, second hand, for the host told the intermediary that he knew Peter Grant as a boy. I turned up at the 'friend's' bungalow: I was greeted by the wife, who said that her husband, Alastair, would be back presently. Of course, I reckoned I knew Alastair as well, until I saw photographs on the piano. Then I began to have doubts, which were confirmed when Alastair, an Inspector of Police, arrived. He said, 'Gosh, it's no you at all,' and I replied, 'No, and it's no you either.' We sorted it all out and a nice time was had by all.

The training programme covered everything from semaphore and heliograph, right the way through to the latest techniques in radio communication, as well as the handling of modern American equipment. One thing annoyed us, for we learned the alphabet in the old British style (Ack, Beer, Charlie, Don), when half way through we had to change to the new American (International) code (Able, Baker, Charlie, Dog).

We were still in Poona at Christmas which was marked by a fire in the mess and riotous behaviour by the Indian staff, celebrating their own festival of Diwali. My servant was in no fit state, next day, for he had been fighting and his clothes were stained in all the possible colours. I passed out with a 'D' rating and returned to the Battalion at Ahmednagar, where we remained for a week or two after New Year. The Don Company officers got into trouble on Hogmanay for we were the duty company and a very important Indian politician, Pandit Nehru, was staying in the fort. Having nothing much to do, we began to play cricket in the great hall and made of lot of noise, which apparently prevented Nehru from sleeping. He complained in the morning, as a result of which we were disciplined.

In a few days we moved down to the sea shore near Bombay – a delightful spot called Juhu with palm-fringed beaches – where we practised assault landings and got used to the water. Swimming was second nature, for everyone had to swim. We sailed every type of craft – including native dug-out, canoes and rafts.

It was here, when Don Company was returning from a route march, Willie McKillop said to me, 'Let's take a short cut across the creek: the tide's out and we can wade across and save six miles' walking.' This was agreed and our two platoons took to the water, but we hadn't gone 200 yards, when the depth of the water necessitated us swimming. There were many good swimmers and many poor ones: the former helped the latter but Willie returned six times to help people in difficulties. All survived, and no equipment was lost, but we didn't noise it abroad, and got into camp as quietly as possible.

Pat McLean, the Adjutant, was lying asleep under a coconut tree, on a Sunday afternoon, when a coconut dropped on his head from a great height. He didn't waken in the usual way but finished up in hospital, where he was checked for concussion, and made a quick recovery. The McLeans are a hard-headed lot.

In the evenings when free we would travel into Bombay, very often on the local buses, for a city always has attractions for soldiers. We then moved to Bhiwandi on foot, which entailed marching for miles alongside a straight, six-foot water pipe. This had mesmeric effect on the troops and many fell out, but we had no option but to march on to our destination, where we stayed for only a few weeks before moving by transport to Mahableshwar (a hill station some 50 miles from Poona).

The road from Poona was narrow and steep, winding its way upwards by a series of hairpin bends. On arriving at the summit we found the whole area covered in very thick jungle, criss-crossed by roads for communication. This was the hot season retreat of white people from Bombay. There were hotels, bungalows and a small bazaar. Our area was in the middle of this jungle. We were not provided with shelter, but each and every officer and soldier made himself a shelter to sleep in, consisting of a bed made from bamboo, with a groundsheet laced across in the form of a bed. Over-head was another groundsheet or waterproof, covered with foliage to give camouflage, and a mosquito net was slung between the two, and a bedroll completed the sleeping arrangements. Washing and toilet facilities were fashioned in a similar manner, as was the officer's mess: all of bamboo and leaves.

The jungle was very thick and one got lost very easily, but soon we acquired a knack for homing back on our company or platoon area. Training took the form of moving through jungle, using the compass, learning about sources of food and drink, and taking precautions against poisonous fruits, berries and snakes. The worst enemy was the rain, for it tanked down unmercifully, and it was nearly impossible to get dry. Of course the natives were always helpful. The Indian *dhobi* (washerman) can work miracles. He will take your clothes, wash them, dry them by some magic, iron them and deliver them back within hours if necessary: always correct because each garment has your own individual *dhobi* mark, which never fades.

On occasion, a few of us would hire a gharry and go to the hotel for a meal. There, we would indulge in high jinks, and it was on such an occasion that, after singing a few Scots songs, I was invited along with my pals to join a party of civilians, the leader of which turned out to be a Highlander, as was his wife. They were joint owners and editors of the *Indian Onlooker*, a society magazine for India, on the pattern of the *Tatler*. They invited us to their home in Bombay when on leave, and arranged with All India Radio for me to sing my Hielan songs over the air, for the enjoyment and otherwise of the troops and the rest of India. There was also a golf course, which was very sporty. The greens were called browns, being fashioned out of hard, baked sand.

On returning home from one of these visits to the hotel on foot, it was pitch dark, as only a tropical night in the jungle can be. Suddenly the two on the far side of the road disappeared: there was a crashing and thumps and we realized that they had fallen off the road and dropped, a long way down a steep hillside. We knew they had reached a ledge or something from the groans and pleas for help. We had no light and no idea how steep was the cliff, but by some means or other some of us got down to the fallen, while others went in search of light which they brought in the form of a *butti* lantern, used by the *chokadar* or watchman from a nearby bungalow. With the help of this meagre light and a lot of swearing, heaving and shoving, we got the fallen back up this nearly perpendicular bank on to the road. They were only bruised, no bones broken, and were able to carry on back to camp, after a contribution of a few annas to the *chokadar* for the use of his equipment. But on getting back to the camp area we found that we were very hungry and tried to seek out the mess, where we knew there was food and drink stored in large baskets. Making our way quietly through the jungle towards a light which we knew was the mess, we halted in the shadow and thicket surrounding the mess area. There was a scene which shook us to the core. Sitting by the open mess basket in the light of a couple of lanterns were two or three of our batmen and a couple of cooks, pouring out drinks, having a jolly time with great laughter, because they were recording their drinks to their officers. 'Put that one down to Grant, Swanson, McKillop,' and so on. What could we do but retire quietly through the jungle to our bunks? There are occasions when that sort of tact is better than creating a fuss.

There was an invitation to a party at the palace of the nearby Raja of Wai. Off we went and were given tea and shown his cheetahs and hawks: this was followed by a sumptuous meal and an ample supply of drink. Our hats ('Balmorals') were hanging in the hall and, on preparing to leave, we found that some of them were missing. Willie McKillop missed his and was righteously indignant when he realized that it was the Raja himself who was wearing it. He had to be physically restrained, but in the end all was resolved and we were able to beat a peaceful retreat to our jungle *charpoys*.

The Commander in Chief, India, was visiting the area. A march past and inspection of selected troops was arranged and I was delegated to command a contingent representing the Brigade and led them in the march past, to be complimented in the usual way afterwards.

Most days it rained because it was the season of monsoon. Sometimes the rain would clear early, to be followed by a lovely sunny day. The Indians love the monsoon: it seems to lubricate their joints and the heat afterwards puts a lift in their step, as they parade about with umbrellas ever at the ready.

Then it was back down to the plains, and a tented camp at a place called Galunche. Here the emphasis was on education and courses. Having qualified as a signal officer I was seconded to the camp of the Worcester Regiment, who were one of the other two Battalions in Fifth Brigade, the Second Dorsets being the third. I was in charge of a Brigade signal course for other ranks. I enjoyed my six-week stay with the Worcesters: Johns, Thompson and Brierley were great characters, as were others who gave the Battalion the flavour of the Territorials, to which it belonged. They loved to play cards, and our schools went on well into 'the wee sma hours'.

One day, however, I was called over to our own Battalion HQ, before the CO, who told me that there was a request for me to sing on All India Radio. He was prepared to grant me leave of absence to go down to Bombay, if I so desired. I did and, after rehearsing for a week (very difficult because we were in a tented camp), I duly reported to the radio station and in the morning had an hour or two's practice with an accompanist. In the afternoon I performed live and was assured that the soldiers heard me loud and clear all over India. I was pleased to accept a small cheque for my services, and duly made my way back to Galunche to face a lot of chaffing and leg pulling. I subjected my brother officers to a rehearsal of the whole programme that night in the mess and they didn't mind.

Shortly after – with Angus Mackay, Ian Swanson and Willie McKillop – I went on leave to Bombay, to the Taj Mahal Hotel. We swam and played golf and snooker at the Wellington Club or the Cricket Club. If we had sponsors – which we always had, for our friends were the MacRaes and the Alexanders who were very influential people – we would meet at the yacht club. We went to the Scots kirk to hear Kenny MacIntosh, the minister, who hailed from Drumnadrochet, and visited his family.

After our return, the Battalion was visited by General Cristisin: a corps commander and a Cameron. It was known that he spoke Gaelic and so, while he was inspecting the officers, I was able to exchange a word or two with him in the 'old language'.

The Army seldom misses a trick. The monsoon was weakening and off we went to rehearse assault landings from the sea. Down to our old friend Bombay we went and in due course we boarded an assault ship named the *Dilwari*, in which we sailed out into the Indian Ocean. On board we were briefed on landings on offshore islands, thinly held by the enemy. We would embark on landing craft by platoons some mile or so off shore and when we hit the shallows, would dash out of the craft, up the beach, and make for the forming-up point, or otherwise depending on whether the landing was opposed or not. Sixteen Platoon, with me in command, clambered down the nets into the landing craft which was rising and falling about twelve feet at a time in the swell. It was about four in the morning and we would land before dawn. Off we went, towards the shore, with a Royal Indian Navy officer at the helm and in due time approached the shore. This had been rehearsed so when the front flap was lowered, with a clattering of chains, I would give the order to charge out through the inner steel doors, followed by my platoon, and up the shore. This I did, but there was no shore. I sank into the dark waters of the ocean and in due course rose to the surface in time to miss the rear propellers of the craft pass in front of me. I could see the outline of the shore and started to swim towards it, eventually reaching it still in full marching order. My platoon, ashen faced, were peering into the darkness, relieved to see me arrive. They, of course, had not followed me into the drink, but stayed put until the craft really hit the shore. There were some hard words all round, especially with the naval officer, but no time to argue so off we went. It was noon before I dried out in the tropical sunshine.

Lt Col Peter Saunders MC was now in command of the Battalion and it was at this point that he led us down to the jungle near Belgaum. This was real jungle, with high forest trees and thick secondary growth underneath. Peter Saunders was a hunter in the Indian tradition and knew the flora and fauna of these parts. We set ourselves up to meet the conditions enforced by our environment and entered into the spirit of jungle warfare, learning all about the lore of that sort of countryside. There were confrontations with bears, and a man-eating tiger was reported to be killing people at a nearby village. A *machaan* was built in a tree and housed a nightly watch, held by a rota of officers taking it in turn to sit up there with a native *shikar*. I took my turn, but nothing happened during my stint, looking down in the gloom at the poor old goat tethered to a tree. But one night he came and was despatched, to the great rejoicing of the villagers.

I went on a reconnaissance with MacDougal, my batman, into a remote area, when suddenly I saw great heaps of steaming dung in blocks the size of a loaf: elephants. They were nowhere to be seen, but it would be most unhealthy to stand around so we beat a hasty retreat to the safety of our jeep.

The new year was approaching and Angus Douglas, the senior major after the 21/C, decided that there would be a celebration to mark Hogmanay. He had made friends with the local Freemasons in Belgaum, who let him have the use of Temple for the night. A feast was arranged and Atholl Brose was prepared. There was singing, dancing, piping and the honoured guests were made welcome. After taking in the New Year in traditional style, with Highland honours, we all adjourned to the temple itself, walked round the square with due decorum and returned to the celebrations in the hall, the tables having been cleared by now.

On New Year's Day, the local regiment, the Maharatta Light Infantry, put on a *Tamasha* which can only be described as a military spectacle. Our main contribution was through the pipe band, which was in first-class trim and always capable of giving a good account of itself. The Drum Major was Sergeant Major Haggart and although he may have imbibed heavily he was still able to catch the baton after hurling it up in the air.

Even after several weeks' stay in the jungle the monkeys would come over just before nightfall high above in the trees and urinate from a great height, giving the impression that the evening breezes brought in with them a drizzle of rain.

We were now clad in jungle green. Everything we wore was of this colour: our underclothes were dyed green, as were handkerchiefs and any other white items. Our gaiters and webbing was Blancoed to a matching green colour and our headgear became a slouch hat, after the Australian style but modified for us and bearing the appropriate flashes of tartan for the regiment and the cross keys for the division.

We felt we were now really ready in every way to meet our adversaries, the so-far unconquered Japanese Army. Part of the Division, the Sixth Brigade, had been sent down to the Arakan front to get first-hand combat experience of the Nip and had found him to be a particularly astute jungle fighter, but as soldier to soldier we were quite capable of putting a stop to his ambitions.

I had set up a very efficient system of inter-company warning systems for jungle warfare, to operate particularly at night to give warning with least possible noise if any enemy approached, and to enable a stand-to to be effected without their knowledge. This was to prove very useful later.

Back we came to Ahmednagar where we were visited by the supremo, Lord Louis Mountbatten, who told us that there would be no action until after the monsoon and that in the mean time we would enjoy a well-earned leave. This was a disappointment, but preparations and rosters were worked out for leave. I went to my well-known haunt of Bombay with Jimmy Hay, Willie McConnachie and Willie McKillop and had a jolly good time visiting friends.

No sooner had we got back to camp than the warning went out to prepare to entrain for the front. The Japs had entered India over the mountain paths, in strength, and were invading Kohima and Imphal, the key points to India in the north-east.

Chapter Six

This was it: no more exercises, no more training, and if ever soldiers were ready for the job in hand we were. All the unnecessary kit was left behind with rear details, in our tin boxes, and only kitbags and small packs were to travel with us to the battle area. A British crack division was to move right across India complete with transport, guns and tanks. As far as I was concerned, it was a case of looking after my men and ensuring that we had everything needed for the fray. I was now Regimental Signal Officer responsible for communications within the Battalion, and communications back to Brigade and to adjacent formations.

We entrained at Ahmednagar station and soon were on our way across the sub-continent, first to Calcutta, then up the river and on to Dimapur – a distant outpost town in Assam and some 2,000 miles away. There were halts at stations for food. The days were spent sleeping, playing cards and talking. It was hot, but these Indian trains were built to deal with climatic conditions to the best of their ability.

We knew what we were in for, and as we looked out on the peaceful countryside, with the peasants toiling in the fields, we wondered whether we would change places with them if the offer were made. But it would not be, and this was our destiny.

So on we trundled, until after the fourth day we were travelling eastward where there was hill country with jungle. This was Assam, the home of the tea planter. In my boyhood days I had heard tales of Assam from the Gollan brothers who had spent their lives there, and had retired to their native Glen in a state of reasonable ease and comfort. Did they ever think that their land would be overrun by the Japanese from many thousands of miles away? Now there were natives guarding the track armed with spears and bows and arrows. Difficult to believe but nevertheless true.

At last the great halt at Dimapur; nothing but a cluster of huts with jungle all around. We were told that the Japanese Army was being held at Kohima, but only just, some 50 miles up the road which eventually led to Imphal. Patrols of the enemy had been spotted near Dimapur so it was a case of deploying straight away, and this we did by companies astride the road and immediately did what we were to do hundreds of times: 'dig in'.

MacDougal, my batman, decided to carry the pick, me the shovel, for the digging of a slit trench was a two-man job, providing shelter for two men. As night descended and we had fed, we were issued with a rum ration. I was given what amounted to a half-gallon flask for my platoon. I had no idea how much the ration per man should be, but I measured it out with my flask top. This proved much too much, and I had great difficulty in keeping my men quiet during the night. They were in good spirits and wouldn't stop talking.

In the morning the trucks stood ready to take us up the 50 miles to the battlefield. So far as I was concerned I travelled in one of the leading trucks with what was Tactical HQ; the CO, Adjutant, IO, SO and Company Commander with the Commander of the Guerilla Platoon in attendance. We joked our way round the never-ending bends, climbing all the way. The speed of the convoy was very slow and we were ever watchful, for soon the sound of guns assailed our ears: muffled thuds at the start, but increasing as the debussing area got closer.

So it was that the vehicles came to a halt and the order to debus was given. All around were the implements of war: field guns were being fired and everyone was behaving in a determined manner, confident in their own ability. Being a British Division we had tended to be isolated from the mainstream of the Indian Army but here we soon realized that we were fighting shoulder to shoulder with Indian formations which in the main were similar to the British. The Indian Division was divided into three Brigades, each with three Battalions of infantry: usually one British, one Gurkha and one Indian Battalion per Brigade.

The Tactical HQ was quickly called forward to a spot where the Brigadier was and which gave a commanding view of the battlefield. To the left was the centre of the conflict, the village of Kohima (or town, rather, because it was the centre of government for a large area of Assam). The fiercest fighting was for the Resident's bungalow, which controlled the main road and where the Royal West Kents were locked in battle with the Japanese across the Resident's tennis court: in spite of all the Nipponese efforts to dislodge them, they had held their positions notwithstanding enormous casualties. The Brigadier explained the tactical situation in the open, although shells were falling all around, one of which had already killed the Roman Catholic Padre, the Revd O'Callaghan, a very popular man. The Brigadier then indicated that those of us who were not directly involved in the orders at the moment could take shelter under the tanks which were all around.

Our area was to be a long ridge overlooking the main

road, on the other side of which, and about 200 yards away, was a knoll, which was thought to be held in strength by the Japs. Off we went through the Brigade Box at Zubsa and on to the ridge where the Battalion was parcelled out in companies, the ground rising up all the time to join the main mountain range behind us.

Arriving at our destination we immediately dug in and set up communications and prepared for battle. Across the road we could see the knoll but no sign of life or movement. The whole area was wooded but the branches and leaves had been stripped by shelling and bombing, and where the British formations were the gaunt stumps of trees were bedecked with parachutes which had carried food and stores from the sky, in an endeavour to keep the forward formations supplied; sometimes impossible to do by road.

On the second day, MacDougal came to me and said that he and his mates had discovered a dump of tinned fruit and meat: you name it, it was there. What would I fancy? I selected fruit and Libby's condensed milk, which was duly brought, consumed and enjoyed. An order came down from Army to the effect that the food and ration dump had been pillaged and if the culprits were caught they would be court martialled.

That night, about eight o'clock, the Brigade box which was about half a mile behind us burst out in a blaze of rifle, machine gun, mortar firing. Bullets whizzed over our heads and tracer lit up the sky in all directions; some of it vertical. Suddenly there appeared at my slit trench the Commanding Officer, Peter Saunders.

'Come with me, Peter,' says he. 'We're going round the whole Battalion to warn them: on no account must they fire until they see the whites of the eyes of the enemy.'

Off we went in the darkness with this pandemonium

going on some quarter of a mile east of our position. From time to time we would be challenged and stopped, but always the warning was, 'Don't shoot until you can see and identify your enemy'. We passed through all the company areas, and returned to our own slit trenches, by which time the hullabaloo to our rear had subsided. Next morning the truth emerged. It wasn't clear whether it was a Japanese patrol that had tried to enter the perimeter or a herd of cattle: whatever it was, the trigger-happy soldiery, mostly Indian, had opened up, shooting indiscriminately. There were casualties caused by the firing, one of whom was one of our own officers: the popular and clever Willie MacMillan, or Willie Mac as he was affectionately known.

It was clear that no progress could be made until the Japs holding the knoll on the other side of the road from our position were moved; and so a battle, our first, was arranged. A and C companies would attack the hill and occupy it. Patrols were sent out and it was clear that the position was strongly held by the Nips, who were dug into bunkers and foxholes (this accounted for the absence of movement in the daytime). The troops involved moved off the hill, down across the road to the starting line where they waited in readiness. I was by the telephone exchange, near to the Brigadier and our CO, to ensure that communications were kept open both by line and radio, although for the purposes of the battle, there was radio silence. Down came the fighter bombers, dropping their loads on the knoll and followed up with a baptism of strafing before departing over the mountains whence they came. Then the guns opened up from the whole divisional artillery. We had some experience of the guns on exercises but nothing like this: shells rained down to the roar of the British artillery like a super thunder. This was the sign for the troops to move forward.

The guns lifted when the troops were about 50 yards from their objective, to be followed by close covering fire from machine guns, mortars and tanks. Then there was nothing left but for the infantry to charge with bayonets gleaming in the sunshine, firing at their targets and doing what they had been trained to do for four years.

There were many deeds of heroism. C Company Commander fell with a bullet in the shoulder leading his company, but his sergeant major was an inspiration to all, thrashing about with a samurai sword taken from his first victim, the Japanese Commander. Twenty minutes later it was all over. Cameron Hill, as it was now named, was in our hands and it was a case of holding the position, securing the ground beyond and consolidating.

The road to the beleaguered Royal West Kents was open and they were relieved, what was left of them, by our own Sixth Brigade, and in particular the Second Dorsets, who were to continue this terrible eye-to-eye battle across the tennis courts.

It could truly be said that the Japanese Imperial Army had suffered its first defeat: small, perhaps, by global standards, but the Camerons' tails were up and our sporrans akimbo.

The first gallantry awards arrived, among them a DCM for Tommy Cook and an MC for David Graham.

The battle was now beginning to take shape. The Japanese were punching at the centre while on their right they had occupied point 5120, the Naga Village, and moved out along the escarpment to Merema: on their left the escarpment rose ever upwards, from Kohima to Jotsoma and beyond. Having taken Cameron Hill, the Battalion was given mules and ordered to proceed up the ridge to Merema; first crossing, with their mule transport, the deep valley and then climbing the hog's back towards the village of Merema. It was a new experience to depend on mules as carriers, but it was extraordinary how they could negotiate the steepest and most intracticable of ridges, screes and gulleys (*kuds*, as they were known in India). We proceeded on foot, fighting our way upward, and eventually held the ridge below Merema in the form of an oval, with each company forming its own Zareba. We were there for a few days, patrolling upwards to Merema and outwards.

One day I went on a visit round the companies and was sitting with Dave Davidson, chatting away in his B Company headquarters, when the warning went out that we were being attacked. Everybody took to their slit trenches but Dave just sat there yawning and drinking his *piala* mug of tea. They are cool customers these Edinburgh lawyers: I had known Dave at Edinburgh University. MacDougal and I then made our way back to HQ in the form of a two-man fighting patrol, for, when you left the company area, you were in no man's land. This tended to be the pattern of the campaign: no such thing as a front line. You were liable to attack from any quarter.

Then we all moved off as a Battalion, with our mules, to the main road. One company turned left and confronted the Japs in Merema, while the rest of us turned right and, in a slow but steady advance, fought our way to a point at the foot of the hill on which Naga village stood: 5,120 feet above sea level, but about 1,000 feet above our position. This was a jungle area which offered more cover than we had had, but meant that we had to be particularly vigilant. For instance, I was talking to one of my corporals when suddenly his face went grey and he slumped on the ground. He was alive, but a bullet had gone through the soft part of his throat. Fortunately he survived, but the sniper was really trying for the officer. Within a minute, a fighting patrol went out, and about half an hour later brought back the body of the Jap marksman.

It was here that our friends the Naga tribesmen came into their own. They were hillmen like ourselves and lived in villages on the tops of hills and mountains. They commuted daily to their paddy fields, down in the valleys, carrying baskets or creels on their backs. The head men of the villages wore red cloaks or blankets and were easily recognizable. They willingly offered their services as porters because they did not like the Japanese who were inclined to kick them around. They still carried spears although the practice of head-hunting was only still pursued in the more remote areas of Nagaland. They were sure-footed and made excellent stretcher bearers, for, in the country we were now operating, there were no roads or even trucks for vehicles and everything had to be transported by humans or mules.

The clear objective for us now was to occupy point 5120, the Naga village, for which purpose patrols were sent out up the hill to reconnoitre a route up there. It appeared that the village and the remaining area at the top was occupied during the day, but at night the Japs came off the crest and returned to their lying-up area, at the foot, leaving standing patrols to cover any possible approach to the top. It was decided that the village should be taken and held by two battalions – ourselves and the Worcesters – and the assault should be carried out at night. Sand shoes were dropped by parachute. These we exchanged for our boots, which were left behind in a dump with rear details. At midnight we moved stealthily, by companies and in single file, ever upwards, through wooded country. In front were the guerilla platoon to deal with any opposition which they did silently and without hardly holding up the advance upwards. I was with this group, led by Neil White, because I was given the job of directing the companies and their soldiers to their allocated positions when we reached the top.

Dawn was just breaking when we got to the top and MacDougal and I stopped and started directing the troops to their areas: as I looked into their eyes, they appeared sightless and glazed. These were the faces of men who were going into battle and in their minds and eyes was one thought: to kill or be killed. As the light increased, the stream of men coming up seemed never ending, but at last it finished and everybody began consolidating their positions by digging in. I had a wonderful position on the top of a tower overlooking the whole Kohima valley, but quickly realized that there was no future there, being too exposed, so we formed a small bunker in the shelter of old broken-down walls, for the whole of the village was flattened by shelling.

About 7 o'clock I could see movement in the valley below and passed the word back so that everybody stood to. I personally fired on what appeared to be a patrol moving in our direction then all hell was let loose, for the Japs were advancing on the hill from all sides. Shells were dropping on our positions and, before long, all the Battalion area was being attacked. But there was also another enemy – the monsoon. Down came the rain in torrents, so we were soaked most of the time, and still fighting in our sand shoes.

One night, it was decided to move the Battalion further west of Naga village, on to positions that we were unable to hold after the first day. Our present positions would be taken over by the Worcesters. We formed up at midnight and moved off. Down came the rain, the thunder roared and, worse still, the lightning lit up the whole area, so that the element of surprise was lost: we could clearly be seen in the flashes of bright light, so whenever there was a flash the Jap machine guns opened up. It was no good, so back we went to our former dug-outs.

It was difficult to keep us supplied, because everything had to be brought in by porter, which necessitated a strong fighting escort, so we were augmented from the air, by parachute drops: here, it was often a battle with the Japs as to who would get to the drop first. Likewise, the wounded were mounting up and had to be transported, manually and at night, by the same native porters and, of course, supplied with a strong escort. On one of these occasions the wounded party was ambushed and the officer in charge killed. In the party, returning to base, was a dental officer, who immediately took command, and by good example and initiative put the attacking Japs to flight and brought the convoy back to base without further casualties. For his gallant conduct, he was awarded the MC.

The days passed into weeks, and still the rain came down in buckets. The enemy continued to attack and use every possible ruse to dislodge us, with great loss of life. One Sunday night, Padre McLauchlan held a church service for those of us who were in the vicinity: this was how he operated, with short services wherever possible. After the service I retired with some of my men to our dug-out which had a roof propped up by large storage baskets of grain. These baskets were full and were about five feet high by four feet diameter. I heard the shell coming and plunged between two baskets from the sitting position. There was the crack above us and I felt a sharp sensation in my arm. When I extracted myself, three of my men were dead and others, like myself, wounded. Help was quickly on hand and we were able to get the wounded out to a place of greater safety, for more shells were dropping. When all was settled I made my way to the Field Dressing Station where my wound was dressed and my arm put in a sling. We had suffered a serious blow because there were three NCOs among our signallers dead or wounded. The Intelligence Officer Johnny McNaught was also killed by the same shell, or another very close at the same time. Johnny was a young man of unusual genius who had a distinguished career in front of him as a writer and dramatist.

After treatment I had to find a place of shelter for the night, and this was in Padre McLaughlan's slit trench where I shared his pipe during fitful waking hours of the night. The morning came to reveal the shambles, when we sorrowfully buried our dead and did our best for the wounded. The CO and I were reluctant for me to go back to the base hospital because we were running short of officers and the maintenance of good communications was of a very high priority.

Anyway, with the help of a new thing, the antibiotic cream, I was able to go about my duties with a sling, using the other arm for self-defence if the occasion demanded, for it wasn't all battle: there were long, tedious periods when you sat around, slept, ate, read (if there was anything to read) and talked. A great argument developed: how to solve Pythagoras' Theorem and, although I had a degree in mathematics, nobody would accept that my solution was the right one, nor anyone else's either. I suppose this was due to the frame of mind you develop under a state of siege.

But we were winning. The daily or nightly attacks, although still pressed home, were diminishing in their ferocity, and the ring round the Naga village was breaking at points and supplies were coming in regularly from down below. These included our boots, which were particularly welcome, for we had sloshed around in sand shoes for over a week and they were by now in a tattered state, and our feet were beginning to rot. The boots were placed in dumps and the problem of finding our own, or even pairs, was nearly impossible. Some had to settle for different sizes and, I believe in one or two cases, for two boots for the same foot. This would have presented a problem to the tracker, for, in the case of the Japanese, we were able to trace their footprints because they were cloven; their boot or shoe had a separate space for the big toe.

Although the air was dominated by our Spitfires and Hurricanes, the Japs were able to give us the odd strafing. One day, when things were quiet, I proceeded a short way down the hill below my slit trench to relieve myself, together with my Sten gun and my spade. Seated comfortably, I looked up to admire the acrobatics of a fighter plane which I thought was one of ours. As it turned, I caught the sight of a red blob on its wings, followed by streams of bullets from its guns in our direction. I was no great sprinter but the speed with which I regained my slit trench would have justified my inclusion in the peacetime Olympics. I pulled up my trousers in my own time in the trench.

One of the great difference between ourselves and the enemy was that, even in the midst of battle, the British observe hygiene rules by relieving themselves in a place other than where they live and eat, whereas the Japs just did it in the foxhole where they lived and ate. We thought this very uncivilized of them.

We were beginning to know more about our enemy, as the days went by. We realized that they were good soldiers but not better than ourselves. There was no quarter given and they expected none, for although we did our best to get prisoners, none gave themselves up: the only ones we could get were those left behind and severely wounded.

The officers and senior NCOs carried Samurai swords, and used them effectively in close combat, but we were much better in the use of arms and our training in self-defence was superior to their judo or jujitsu. They had no built-in desire to survive, for to die for the Emperor was the greatest blessing that could happen to a soldier. We did not share this view. Every Japanese soldier wore a flannel belt, decorated by little red knots, every one of which was sewn on by relatives and lady friends.

An interesting feature was revealed when we came across a Japanese mess basket containing the finest and most delicate hand-painted crockery. All we had was our mess tin and enamel mug. When one considers that this army had advanced over the mountain tracks from Burma into India with only elephant, mule and coolie transport, it is extraordinary that they would bother to bring such refinements of their civilization. On the other hand, their medical services were practically non-existent, and when a soldier was badly wounded he was promptly put out of his misery: this applied equally to their prisoners.

The battle had gone so well that it became possible to relieve us on the mountain top. The Worcesters had not joined us at the top, they had consolidated the village and then took up positions on the slope up to ensure our supply route. On the appointed day for the withdrawal we handed over to a battalion of Punjabi. Each man took over a position from one of ours and we in turn made our way down the slope we had cleared, through the Worcester lines to a bussing area, where we climbed into lorries to return to the Brigade area at Zubsa for a meal, bath and change of clothes.

I was seated in my bath, which was half an oil drum, cut lengthwise and filled with a few cans of hottish water, heated in large containers over wood fires, all in the open.

Suddenly round the corner came Sergeant Pat McLeod – the signal Sergeant at Brigade HQ, a regular soldier of the Royal Corps of Signals and, like myself, a native of Glen Urquhart – who saw to my signal requirements. He exclaimed, 'Good God, Pe . . ., Sir! I thought you were dead!' We were agreed that I wasn't and he produced a substantial measure of good Canadian rye whisky. When we were fed and watered, we moved off for our rest area.

We had kept ourselves clean, despite the shortage of water on Kohima village. Our ration was two pints per day, for all purposes. For washing I would put a couple of eggcups-full into my tin hat, lather my face and shave then use the same water for washing my face afterwards then any other part of the anatomy that needed attention, particularly the feet. I always endeavoured to keep my water-bottle full and tablets were issued to ensure that any bugs which might be prowling about were neutralized.

To fight the threat of malaria, which is induced by the mosquito bite, we took one mepacrine tablet every day. This was a strict requirement, and failure to do so, when established, was dealt with, in accordance with the Army Act. As a result of taking these mepacrine tablets our skins assumed a yellow tinge not unlike those of the chaps we were fighting.

The area we occupied was to the west and higher up the slope of the mountain where we had first dug in, prior to the battle of Cameron Hill, near Jotsoma. The whole area was well dug in with most sophisticated bunkers, and had formed part of the main defensive area on the right of the Kohima stronghold. It had been occupied before us by the 17 Indian Division, and the bunkers were clean and tidy.

Bertie Harvey, the Adjutant, shared one of these bunkers with me and very comfortable we made ourselves, although

I think the British soldier prefers the open air to the claustro-phobia of a bunker. Patrols were constantly sent out to keep an eye on the enemy positions, but it was only a short spell of three days' rest, when we could sit back and take stock and make plans for the next move.

I was in a strong position, so far as my wireless sets were concerned. Not long before we left for the front, our radio sets (send and receive) – the British 14 set – were replaced by an American one which was very similar but not so robust. We had to hand in our old sets, but I never got round to doing so, and it was the wisest non-compliance ever, for I had twice as many sets as the other battalions. The wastage rate was very high and replacements difficult to come by, but not for me, for I had the old British sets to fall back on and they never let us down.

The problem of the men, however, was different. My platoon had suffered relatively high casualties and no re-placements were available so we had to make do. The regi-mental records of the time say, 'While recognition cannot come to all, every officer and man shares the credit which has already accrued to the Regiment and pride that its name stands so high. Specific tribute must be paid, none the less, to the Battalion Signals Platoon under the command of Cap-tain P J T Grant, which combined a consistent record of hard work and efficiency with the highest proportional casualty rate in the Battalion.' I had been promoted to Captain during the battle on Naga village, but there was no time for cele-bration.

We were warned that on the morrow we would move. I was sent down the road to meet and escort back a cadre of reinforcements. On meeting them I gathered them all around and addressed them. They had come from the Cameron depot in Inverness, but there were also men from the RA anti-aircraft regiments and some from the navy. Anyway, I assured them that they were welcome and once a Cameron always a Cameron. But I recognized a very young, pink-cheeked boy, who was a Cameron recruit. John McLeod Fraser, the grocer Tom's son from Lewiston, Drumnadrochet. I hadn't seen him for many years, but made him welcome. I couldn't assure him of a place of safety, however, for on the morrow he was to make his first kill.

Chapter Seven

We moved from our comfortable quarters on the hill, and after a short march we were transported by lorries to a spot above the District Commissioner's bungalow. From there we made our way upwards to the Aradura spur which crossed the road and passed through the Dorset lines to confront the enemy, who was holding them up in some strength. An attack was laid on under the direction of Major Angus Douglas, 21/C of the Battalion. It was carried out in the traditional Highland style, with the stealthy move up, then the charge, with the pipes playing the advance.

No record of the Camerons would be correct without reference to the pipers' role; not only did they provide entertainment and the beat for the march, but also the inspiration for the advance. But in his hour of triumph, Angus Douglas died: he was a Cameron of the old school, gentleman, sportsman, horseman and supreme raconteur, but above all a true soldier.

The situation was difficult, for the rain poured down and the tanks could not reach our new positions because of the mud. Snipers were all around and the Japs were still dominating our newly-won position on the Araduma Spur.

An amusing thing happened, showing how in the midst of war the Army can still deal with the little details. When I had my bath and a change of clothing back at Zubsa, I had omitted to remove from my tunic and trousers the escape devices which we had sewn into our clothing. This I had reported and a search was made through the hundreds of dirty trousers and tunics until they were discovered and sent forward for me to sew into my fresh uniform of jungle green.

The pursuit was now on to chase the Jap back along the Imphal road and relieve the sorely invested garrison in the Imphal plain. So back we went to our mules and took to the mountains which rose steeply on both sides of this long and tortuous road. There were few paths and the jungle was very thick. The villages were perched on the highest points. All stores and equipment were carried by the Naga porters and the mules and it was a case of finding the easiest approach to a village, and then ascertaining whether it was in enemy hands or not. It was an unrelenting game of hide and seek. The villages offered a bit of shelter in their huts, which housed the livestock as well as the families, but there was little comfort in the houses, because of the fleas which had such powerful jaws. I remember the MO, Peter Barkey, sitting on a rock in the morning sunshine, picking these little beasties out of his shirt, and counting them by the hundred. Being brought up in the Highlands, I enjoyed the mountains.

Over the radio came the message that Allied troops had landed in Normandy. The second front was on. But for us it was slog on. At night everyone took their turn to keep watch for two hours in turn, while the rest slept. The night sounds in the jungle comprise a cacophony of strange and eerie grunts, groans, whistles, hisses, catcalls, growls and coughs, from every sort of animal which takes the opportunity of the night to replenish its stomach and perform its natural functions. To pick out from all these sounds the approach of the enemy took a lot of listening, looking and smelling, for all the senses had to be alerted.

Still the rain fell and we never removed our clothes

or boots: our slit trenches would be half-full of water by morning.

The Sixth Brigade, which was operating on the main road, was held up at Viswema, a fairly large village, and we were called in to help. We descended on the slopes above the village with the object of clearing the overlooking territory of the enemy. A bloody battle ensued; early in the morning, under heavy machine-gun fire, I got myself into a slit trench occupied by a dead soldier and for over two hours could not advance because every time I lifted my head a shower of bullets rained over me. When night came the CO decided that the only way to shift the Jap from this hillside was to get above him and drive him off it from a higher position. So at about 3 a.m. we moved off up the bed of what can only be described as a Highland burn, complete with boulders and a raging torrent. Up we went, slipping and sliding, soaked to the skin, but silent.

About an hour before dawn we emerged at the top of the mountain and spread out by companies which were now reduced to not much more than 30 to 40 each. We had a quick, cold breakfast before starting to move down. The point we had reached was between nine and ten thousand feet, and the air was rarefied. In due course, as dawn was breaking, we spotted the Japs beginning to stir themselves and we put in an attack, supported only by our own mortars and a couple of machine guns from the Manchesters. The Nip was really taken with his pants down and fled in confusion. We followed on, moving and firing, until, with a final charge in the glorious sunshine of an Alpine-like slope, full of flowers and plants, we threw the Jap off the ridge and the threat to Viswema was over. The Royal Welsh cleared the village and all faces turned westwards, towards ever-towering mountains.

In the exhilaration of the day one felt that here we were on the frontiers of civilization, pushing back the threat of barbarism to the peaceful people of India, but it was a long way to Burma.

Our next objective had a very eastern name: Mao Sang Song, the highest point on the road from Kohima to Imphal, so back we went to our mountain tracks and, a few days later, we were in sight of Mao. Our role there was to carry out a left hook, while the main force made the frontal attack on this bastion. To do this we had to clamber down the very steep side of a ravine, cross a raging torrent at the bottom of the valley, climb up the other side and move, unseen, along the top of the ridge which ultimately led down to the village of Mao Sang Song. All this at night.

The food situation had got quite bad by now. The normal breakfast was porridge and bacon or sausage: the latter being a particularly revolting soya variety. We liked our porridge because it was made in the proper Scottish style, while our neighbours the Worcesters hated it because they really did not know how to make it. Being friends, we used to give them some of our bacon ration for a measure of their oatmeal. The time came, however, when there was no bacon, only oatmeal. The result was that we went into battle merrily, with our bellies full of porridge, while the poor Worcester lads went in with a slice of bread for breakfast. We therefore lent them a few of our cooks to make proper porridge and soon the men from Worcestershire were marching forward on porridge.

A reconnaissance of the route down and across the valley, up the other side to the starting point, was made, and a white tape was set up to show us the route. As it was night time, the method of proceeding was to hold on with one hand to the back of the man in front. We set off at midnight and the descent was not unusual, there was sporadic gunfire, and suddenly a shell burst not very far from us with the result that my batman, Private MacDougal, leapt on my back as he was the next behind me.

'What's the matter, MacDougal?' says I.

'Ma nerves are all to fuck if you want to know, Sir,' was the brief reply, but we kept on our downward path swearing and sliding.

When we reached the bottom there was the river to cross, on fallen trees, and there is nothing I dislike more than walking on a tree trunk over swift running water, particularly in the dark. The climb up the other side was on a bare hillside, till eventually we reached our objective and made the deployment to advance on Mao, synchronized with that of Sixth Brigade, and by noon it was all over. The objective, 6,000 feet above sea level, was captured.

Two days later we advanced on to Maram, where the Worcesters, now full of porridge, made a dashing attack and took the objective to let the armour through. Next day, the 22 June, our tanks met up with the Imphal garrison tanks and the road to Imphal was clear. Alec Leckie, the Quartermaster, brought up the bivouacs and we settled down to rest. Alas, in the morning I had a temperature of 103° and Peter Barkey diagnosed either dysentery or malaria, and ordered me off to hospital which was back at Kohima. The ambulance was a converted Jeep, driven by a member of the American Field Service, a Quaker organization that did this voluntary work in the theatres of war. I sat in the front with the Yankee driver, while the back was loaded up with three stretchers containing wounded Japanese. All the Japs would or could say was 'Kohima'.

The journey was slow but eventually we arrived at the field hospital. All around were the sick and wounded, evidence of the ferocity of the battle that was still raging and had gone on unremittingly since early April. Although I could walk, I was put on a stretcher and eventually carried shoulder high down steep slopes to a ward where I was bundled into bed and given injections before going into a blissful sleep.

Next morning I felt a lot better, but had to lie back and take things easy. The company was good and there was lots of chat. Next to me was an American who talked incessantly of his New England home, and how, when the war was over, we would both go fishing on his wonderful windswept shore. There was a bottle of beer every day and a large glass of brandy in the evening. After two or three days my temperature was back to normal, and I was allowed up. I walked out and actually climbed the hill to the Naga village where we had fought so valiantly. It was a scene of desolation but, being the tropics, the grass and foliage was growing rapidly, and the natives were settling into their huts.

Next day I decided to return to my unit which was now in Imphal. I went up onto the road and hailed a tank that was making its way over this tortuous route to Imphal. The ride took quite some time and, although bumpy, was most interesting and I was able to point out all the places where interesting confrontations took place. It made me appreciate how fortunate we were to be infantrymen to be free to move about in the open air and not be cramped in a steel box. On the other hand, we did not have the protection of six inches of the aforementioned steel.

This close and mountainous country was very difficult for operating armoured vehicles, for the conning tower lid had to be open: the result of this was that the Jap could leap out from the undergrowth, onto the tower, and slash off the heads of the crew, or even, from a short distance, toss in a grenade. The result was that each tank had to move with an infantry escort to prevent these nasty things happening.

I was dropped off in the Battalion area in Imphal, and received a warm welcome after my three days' absence, during which the road to Imphal had been cleared and the Battalion were now lying back in bivouacs, resting their poor old feet.

We had started off at Kohima with 600 men: we were now about 250 and, obviously, before proceeding forward, would have to be heavily reinforced. Imphal is a small shanty town in the midst of a vast plain which is completely surrounded by hills, from which the Japs had endeavoured to squeeze the life out of the garrison. There is a large lake there, which is inhabited by a wide variety of birds, many of them migratory, and it was a pleasure to watch them come in and fly off, feed, mate, and so on, oblivious to what was going on around them. There was also a bazaar, with goods for sale; not that we provided a great outlet for their merchandise but, at least, it was some sort of return for us to the elementary principles of civilization. We enjoyed ourselves in our simple way, playing cards, throwing dice, writing letters and, fortunately, there was a fair supply of liquor consisting of Indian beer and Canadian whisky. Mariner's Indian Gin was also available in large quantities: this was through the good officers of the NAAFI, the manager of which was from Inverness and was known to Allan McKillop.

Then we were told that we would have to move up to the front for a few days to take over from an Indian division that was going forward against the Japs, who had now reformed and were going to prevent the advance south of the Burmese border and the Chindwin River. I was sent off up there with one or two other officers, to reconnoitre the area that we were to take over. It was held by an Indian Sikh regiment, well dug in and most comfortably accommodated in bunkers. They made us very welcome, and entertained us in a bunker to tea and chapattis – which they baked on a hot stone in a fire on the bunker floor – washed down with rice wine, for the Sikhs have no inhibitions about the consumption of liquor.

A day or two later we moved off and took over the Sikh positions allowing the attacking troops to move through our lines. They turned out to be our neighbours from the Scottish Highlands, the Seaforths. Although we were in a holding role, we were subjected to lots of stick from machine-gun fire until the battle was over and things quietened down.

We followed on down the road towards the Chindwin and held the town of Palel for a few days before pushing on to Tamu. We were now under the command of the 23rd Indian Division and saw more of our Indian comrades. I was busily engaged in digging a slit trench by the side of a stream; there were Gurkhan troops about. When my task was nearly finished and I was resting, a Gurkhan soldier came over to me with a *piala* of tea, offering it with the words, 'Tea, sahib'. I was very grateful. Then on down to Tamu and the Kabaw valley which had such a bad reputation for disease and pestilence. Sure enough, as we probed forward the Japanese lay dead, or dying, by the roadside not from bullets but from disease, and although we were hardened to war, we realized that here we were truly in the valley of death.

Those of the enemy who were not dead were collected as prisoners because we still had not taken any fit men as prisoners; they never surrendered. Neither did we, for it was known that none of our men taken prisoner by the Jap were ever seen again. We literally took hundreds but we were more than glad when the order to return was given, and, jumping into transport, we made our way back to Imphal and onwards back over the now well-known road to Kohima, to a point known as the 82nd milestone on a commanding site at Maram.

We set up camp and were told that we would rest here while another fresh division would continue our fight through the monsoon. Here we indulged ourselves, bathed and read papers. An officers' latrine was built: a double seater with a sheltering roof overhead, looking out over the valley. Down in the river was a plentiful supply of fish, and a rough and ready mess was built from available timber.

While we were driving on from Kohima a memorial stone was being erected on 5120 in the Naga village, to commemorate the gallant fight put up by the 1st Camerons in this great battle which in later years had been recognized by military historians as one of the great battles of history. Allan McKillop, my friend from Inverness, designed it and on the appointed day the whole battalion returned to Kohima to unveil this tribute to our fallen comrades and to read the words below: 'Lochaber no more'. The pipers played their laments, the Padre conducted the service and the last post and reveille sounded through the hills where, months before, the guns had roared. Standing just outside the ring of Camerons were the Nagas, hillmen like us, all dressed in their tribal colours, red predominating, taking part in the service: the moment of ending was the signal for them to break into *Onward Christian Soldiers*. This tumultuous sound from hundreds of warriors – carrying their spears, bows and arrows, and shields – brought tears to the eyes of every Cameron soldier. Standing on the plinth I led the Battalion in singing the *Cameron Men*.

Next day we held a Highland Games in which representatives of all the Scots regiments were pleased to take part. I think the Black Watch won most points but a good time was had by all.

The highlight of the rest-up, however, was leave which was granted to all ranks, so off we went to our selected places, for the most part in a group of three or four. So it was that, whereas some found their way to Ceylon or Srinagar, I and three kindred souls set out for Bombay. After what we had been through anywhere would have been better. We went by jeep to Dimapur, train to Calcutta and then on to Bombay, into a taxi and straight for the Taj Mahal Hotel, grasping the precious bottle of Canadian whisky which was my month's ration and kept secure for the occasion.

Once arrived at the Taj, we were met by the welcoming *kitmagars*. I handed the bottle to one of them who turned and started to mount the steps when he dropped it and it crashed on the marble step where it broke into a thousand pieces with the beautiful golden liquid running down to the gutter. We called him everything we knew in Hindi and English, then turned to the kids who were swarming round the foot of the steps and made the traditional 'pour out' which we did on these occasions.

We had been at war for six months, and now was the occasion to spend our money and have a good time dining, wining, swimming, golfing, sailing, looking up friends and having great fun. The city was full of others like us, all with the same idea. Bombay is a particularly nice city with wide streets for main shopping, where you find sophistication at the Army and Navy stores and many fine jewellers and carpet shops. There are parks and clubs and fine hotels.

The Scots kirk to which we went to hear a fellow Glen Urquhart man, Revd Kenny McIntosh, was very large and beautiful, air-conditioned and, whenever we went there, full to overflowing. There is also a fine university and museum, while in the evening it is a pleasure to walk along the promenade by the sea to the Gateway of India, which was always thronged with all sorts of people taking the air. There is a very good hospital on Malabar Hill – which is of course crowned with the Towers of Silence, the final resting place of the Parsees. The parsees came to India from Persia and are nearly white. They are in the main rich merchants but, owing to their being a separate race in India, tend to be inbred: during the war the rich parents were keen to marry their daughters off to the British to strengthen the blood.

The beaches where we had trained were easily accessible and a day spent down at Juhu was most rewarding.

Chapter Eight

Time to return was approaching and the journey back was long and slow, but we found out that travel by military aircraft was possible; at least to Calcutta. On enquiring at the military airport office, we were told very brusquely that flying was restricted to front-line troops only: what were we? When the Corporal heard that we were from Two Division and 1st Camerons he adopted a most deferential attitude and issued the tickets which had the effect of extending our stay by three days. The Dakota was waiting for its load at the airport, and at 6 a.m. we took off, bleary eyed but happy. India is a big place and at about 11 a.m. we came down for refuelling and lunch in central India, prior to pushing on to Dum Dum at Calcutta. There we climbed into another plane the following morning, which set us down at Dimapur where we had first detrained prior to the battle of Kohima. We were welcomed back at the 82nd milestone camp where our wounded and sick were beginning to rejoin the Battalion along with drafts from all sorts of military, and even naval, establishments in India where there was no longer a need for their specialized services.

To absorb the new recruits and refresh the rehabilitated wounded required a lot of training and this was duly done. With officers being on leave there was quite a lot of standing in during which period I had acted as IO and Adjutant.

A select body of 150 men and 10 officers returned to Kohima one day for the unveiling of the 2nd Division

Memorial: a great stone, standing about twelve to fifteen feet high, roughly hewn from the rock and bearing the words from the Greek: 'When you go home, tell them of us and say that for your tomorrow we gave our today'. A fitting tribute to the men who now lay in the new cemetery where the great battle of the District Commissioner's Bungalow had taken place.

During all of this time, the monsoon was raging and although some days were bright and fair, others poured with rain as it can only do in Assam, one of the wettest parts of the world. The Japs never thought that the 14th Army would fight through the mud of the monsoon: they were wrong and the battle went on relentlessly. Soon it was our turn again, but an outbreak of tick typhus marred the pleasant stay of nearly three months at Maram. This disease is contracted from ticks in the grass and, sad to say, some of our men died from it, although with our modern drugs we were able to deal with the scourge better than the Japs who died in their thousands.

On St Andrew's day we were off again with a rum ration to warm our insides. The first part of the journey was by East African Divisional Transport, and some difficulty was experienced, for it was the habit for the officer or sergeant to sit in front with the driver to map-read or do what was necessary. However, the Africans wanted their own buddies beside them, and stern methods had sometimes to be adopted.

It was about 200 miles to Yazagyo, a former Japanese camp. Here we relaxed and repaired the roads forward. It was nearing Christmas and, as we were due to go forward before long, Christmas was celebrated a week early. There was an issue of beer and spirits. I kept my bottle of whisky for New Year's Eve, Hogmanay, and as we marched along you could hear it clunking to the rhythm of the step.

We advanced over this dry and arid land, from village to village. On one occasion, MacDougal my batman went on a foraging expedition with me to try and secure eggs, chickens or tomatoes: *oos*, *chetoos* or *kayengendas*. We approached a village stealthily and gained the thicket, which usually surrounded these native villages. We could hear screams and laughter from female voices and as we peered through the thick bush we could see, in the middle of the village clearing, a pond in which naked women and children were doing their washing and – sitting on the edge of the pond, idly throwing or casting pebbles at the women – there were half a dozen Jocks from our own regiment. We did not disturb them, but retired and left them to their bit of innocent fun.

We were getting closer, village by village, and now knew that the Japanese were holding the line of the Mu River. On New Year's Eve we were halted prior to our advance to take the defended village of Ledi. Brigade HQ were within close contact and in the evening I sought out Sergeant Pat McLeod at Brigade HQ to give him a drink from my bottle which I had carried so faithfully for the past two weeks. We had a few swigs and I returned with a supply of new batteries for my wireless sets.

Next day we took Ledi, which was lightly defended, but at night when we were consolidating at a crossroads near the village, suddenly there was an alarm that we were being attacked. Everyone went to ground, but I hadn't time to dig a trench; nor had MacDougal. He got into a trench with some others but the only place I could get was into the culvert under the road, for there was firing and bursting of grenades. I got into the pipe head first with my Sten gun in my hands, but it was so narrow that I couldn't manoeuvre. I then heard Japanese voices at the other end of the tunnel, which was about 20 yards long, but could only hope that they didn't see me. They soon departed, for it was now a very unhealthy place for them to be discovered. I was pulled out of the tube by my feet amid a good deal of laughter and banter.

The Mu river was a great barrier, being about 100 yards wide, but we were told that it was fordable in certain places. To get to some of the more remote villages on the River Mu we hired a hundred bullock carts with drivers. These were loaded up with stores and ammunition and the sight of all 100 carts and bullocks trundling along the dusty tracks may have been reminiscent of the advance, a thousand years earlier, of Genghis Khan.

We were kept amused and light-hearted at this time by the arrival of a Canadian officer, Jim Mullholland, who was a member of the Cameron Highlanders of Canada, and who had been present at the Dieppe raid when so many of his countrymen died. He was an expert on regimental history and never missed a chance of going on a patrol or a reconnaissance.

A new method of reconnaissance came into operation at this time. As the country was more open, airstrips were being built by bulldozer excavation, and light planes – and later even Dakotas – could land and take off. The officers involved in the advance would be taken over the ground in one of these two-seater planes, and the sight of these green-faced officers dismounting after a flight was weird. I took part in several of these over the Mu and Irrawaddy, and the pilot would invariably loop the loop prior to landing.

We were informed that there was a ford across the river

at a village called Bitagaya, where the head man pointed out the crossing point. We moved into the water, company by company, each man gripping the pack of the man in front. This was necessary as the current was quite strong, and the river deeper than we expected. When it reached up to my chest, remembering that we held our weapons aloft, out of the wet, I felt a tugging behind me and on looking round in the dark saw the figure of MacDougal horizontal in the water, but still gripping my pack and also held by the man behind him.

'How did you lose your hold, MacDougal?' quoth I.

'My f—g feet were washed away from the bottom,' he replied, for he was only about 4' 10" and very light with it. We struggled on and, still in the dark, landed on the far shore.

We immediately proceeded to take up defensive positions and dig in on what appeared to be the outskirts of a village. Most, if not all, the men took off their trousers to let them dry more easily, for wet clothes are very uncomfortable. While we were digging our trench, suddenly there was the sound of shooting and explosions. I looked up and saw a figure bearing down on us firing an automatic from the hip; I could see the flashes from his gun. I threw down my shovel and grabbed MacDougal's rifle but the round stuck in the chamber. The Jap was on us and flung a grenade in our direction: it went over my head and exploded behind me, a fragment clipping the edge of the CO's nose. By now I had the round in the chamber, took a pot at the running Jap and got him in the knee: over he went and was taken prisoner. We found that the Japanese unit holding this part of the river bank had received a tip-off and had laid an ambush.

As we were entering the water to cross the river we heard

the bell of a temple ring out. The saffron-robed priests are known as *punjis* and the temple itself the *punji chaung*. Now that we were in part of Burma, the religion of the people was mainly Buddhist. On entering the temple after the little battle, we found that a priest was lying dead in a pool of blood, with a dagger in his back. Who committed this foul deed? Was it the Japanese or the local natives? The truth will never be known.

With the crossing of the Mu one other defence line for the Nips had gone, and it was pursuit to Shiwebo, which we were told was strongly held, and which formed the enemy defence line, before the Irrawaddy River itself. The tanks could now deploy but so could the Japs' tanks, and it was most disconcerting to find yourself looking across three or four hundred yards of unbroken flat country at a couple of tanks, not knowing whether they were ours or theirs. The only thing to do was to lie low, in the absence of anti-tank weapons, and hope that they were ours.

It was near here that our friends the Worcesters came a cropper. They were held up by a strongly held Japanese position in a village. It was open flat land all around and the Worcester CO decided on a frontal attack on a battalion front in the grand style. The attack failed: the CO, Adjutant and three Company Commanders were killed along with many others. The result was that our Second in Command, Tom Irvine, had to go over to them as CO and as they were now severely short of officers, he had to take some of ours to fill in, until reinforcements were forthcoming. In the mean time, while they were recouping their losses, the task was given to us, which we did by the well-tried process of fire and movement: a flanking hook together with a spot of artillery and air support.

It was only a few miles to the bank of the Irrawaddy.

The river from bank to bank was well over a mile wide, and a current quite strong. The process of clearing the enemy from the near bank did not take long but, quite evidently, the Imperial Nipponese Army was going to hold the far bank and deny the 14th Army a foothold for as long as possible. Crossing the river was the shortest way to Mandalay, then it was down the plain of Burma to Rangoon.

The Battalion was allocated an area close to the bank of the river, from which one could just see the far bank, but immediately in front was an island or ayot in the river. The bank of the river was high so that our movements could not be seen by the enemy on the other side of the river except, of course, from the air. A plan for the crossing had been devised and active preparations put in hand. It appeared that the assault on our sector should be carried out on a two-battalion front. The infantry would cross in canvas, inflated, coracle-type craft, propelled by oars to ensure silence, in the night. Later, when a bridgehead had been established, the engineers would take or ferry other troops across in flat-bottomed, punt-like craft, with outboard engines, and next day the DUCKWS would cross with heavy equipment such as guns.

There was, of course, a great deal of activity. General Slim came along to have a look at us, as also did the Supremo, Lord Louis Mountbatten; always with a joke for everyone and full of suave urbanity. He had previously been injured when his jeep had gone over the side of a *khud*. The officers went up in the recce plane. I seemed to be unlucky, for on this occasion there was more than usual other air activity between fighters of both sides, but one could see the bank on which we would land: it was steep and sandy, an obstacle in itself, whereas on our side it was a gentle sloping shore or beach, shelving into the water. The idea was for us to paddle around the island, which was now held by our own troops, and then make straight for the cliffs. The ground on the far side was flat and covered with elephant grass, providing cover for their machine guns.

The news came that the Adjutant, Bertie Harvey, had been appointed to a staff job in Intelligence, at Division, and would be leaving the Battalion in a few days. Some time afterwards I was hailed over to where the CO and 21/C Alan Roy were sitting on a log. 'Sporran Jock' – as Angus MacAlister, the CO, was affectionately known by troops and officers alike – said that they had been talking over the matter of Adjutant, and had come to the conclusion that the job should be mine. I was very pleased and told them that I was delighted to accept this ancient and prestigious appointment; that I would do my best to fill the post the post of Captain and Adjutant of the 1st Camerons; and that I would now liaise with Bertie so that the take-over would be as smooth as possible. The Adjutant is responsible for the administration: he writes the battle orders on instruction of the CO, records casualties of all kinds, promotions, and generally sees that everybody knows what is going on. He must strike up and maintain a good relationship with the CO and be able to convey his wishes and intentions to the Company Commanders.

Preparations for the great crossing were complete: a crossing fourteen miles further north, and to the north of Mandalay itself, had been effected and the sound of battle could be heard day and night. We would supply the right hook on that city. So at midnight we sailed out, in our armada of coracles, rowing for all we were worth; each craft trying to keep in touch with the others. It wasn't easy, for the night was dark and the current swift, but after an hour or so we were round the head of the island, which was held by the Royal Welsh Fusiliers who would be watching our progress. On our right the Worcestershires were doing the same but we could hear the rattle of machine guns from that quarter and knew that they had been spotted. So far we did not appear to have been picked out by the Japanese spotters, but not for long. We were right out in the main stream when enfilade fire from the banks opened up. We did not reply, nor could we, but we kept on paddling. Soon our craft and the people in them were being hit, and casualties were mounting, but it was on, on to the bank which was reached first by B Company under Bill Davidson, plus the guerrilla platoon. From then it was a case of getting up the bank and fanning out as more troops came in. We landed, as had been decreed, formed a Battalion HQ on top of the bank and into the side of the bank itself.

The crossing had taken its toll. A Company Commander, John Bain, had gone and our doctor, Peter Barkey, had failed to reach the near bank, so the First Aid Post was set up under the command of the Padre, Frank, who had been sitting beside Peter and who himself had a bullet through his tin helmet. There was a lot of firing on the Company fronts but the Battalion had got across and was clinging on to its foothold despite mounting attacks and shelling. The pioneers hacked out a sloping ramp from the bank down to the river, and before dawn a pontoon with jeeps arrived, followed shortly after by a small armoured bulldozer. But there was no support on our right. The Worcesters had been shot out of the water and were forced to retire, so the only way to reinforce the landing was through our own bridgehead. I was now Adjutant and when dawn came I was sent back over the river to report all the circumstances personally to the Brigadier.

By now the Royal Engineers had got their flat-bottomed boats, with outboards, going, and were ferrying troops across as far as possible. It was a case of running the gauntlet of the Nip machine guns. We realized that the priority for the troops who had got across was to destroy these machine-gun posts and quite clearly they would make every effort to do so. Our guns were busy with targets pointed out by the troops on the spot and would be hoping that ere long they too would be across.

When daylight came the RAF joined in. They, of course, had Canadian and Australian troops under command. I got back across the river and made for Brigade HQ which consisted of a sandbagged pillbox in the middle of a field some quarter-mile back from the riverbank. The journey there on foot seemed simple, except that at the moment of my setting out the Jap artillery opened up on the area and as I proceeded I had to dodge from one shell hole to another as I heard them come over. I could see anxious faces at the Zareba, watching my progress, and as I sprinted the last fifty yards to the sandbags they stretched out their hands and hauled me over. One of them was none other than my friend Sergeant Pat McLeod from the Glen and the other was the Brigadier himself.

I was taken below and given rum and tea and I put the Brigadier, Michael West, and his aides in the picture. He decided that I should tell the same story to the General and so I was pushed over the sandbags again to make my way for a couple of miles to Divisional Headquarters.

I made good speed there for the shelling had eased: I think our gunners had pinpointed them and treated them to a bit of traditional British gunnery. At Divisional HQ all was activity. The General was up front somewhere, so my tale of the landing and consolidation was listened to politely by two staff officers who promised to pass the information on to the General. They then gave me lunch; quite luxurious because it was dished up on an enamel plate. They also put me on a jeep to get me back to the shore where there was now enormous activity. The Worcesters were crossing in DUKWS and I got on one of these and off we went down the beach into the water and off in a state of luxury not known twelve hours before. This time there was no machine-gun fire and soon we were out on to *terra firma*, and while the Worcesters made their way through our lines in the long grass, I reported back to Sporran, who was in an expansive mood by now, having been first across and already planning the break-out towards Ava Bridge. After Ava it would be on to Mandalay, the fabled city of the kings of Burma and of Kipling's song. We were indeed 'on the road to Mandalay'.

Chapter Nine

I settled down with my staff to the sad task of recording and forwarding the casualties, and burying the dead. We were very sad about Peter Barkey, the doctor, who was a great man with forward-looking ideas on the application of medicine, and one who had done a wonderful job with the sick and wounded from Kohima to the crossing. John Bain we didn't find because his whole boatload was dead and washed down the river.

Patrols went out and found that the Japs were holding a line from the great Ava Bridge, the central span of which was down in the river right across our front. The plan devised for us was to swing left on a two-battalion front and advance on the Nip stronghold. The country was flat and we were now confronting the main Japanese Army, withdrawn in depth, who had orders to deny Burma to the British. Everything had to be brought across by water, for it would be some time before the Ava Bridge would be liberated and repaired. Bulldozers had the job of creating a ramp from the water up to the ground level, and then, when space allowed, to fashion out an airstrip. Within a couple of days aircraft were landing and taking off. The Dakota aircraft, which was used in these parts, was the most adaptable and manoeuvrable possible. Then came the armour, which could now perform its proper duty of operating in open ground and was available for the protection of the bulldozer crews who were suffering casualties in these exposed positions, despite the fact that they were partially armoured.

Eventually, the time was right for the advance on the Ava line. Our right flank was protected by an Indian Division which had crossed over the river and pushed out to our south and west. The 2nd Division would advance on Ava and thence on Mandalay. As Adjutant it was now for me to write the battle order, to cover the role of all companies and supporting troops of the Battalion, including the role of the guns and supporting air strikes, and, on this occasion, the tanks.

The infantry would advance on a two-battalion front, supported by tanks. The line of advance was about two miles of a front, with three companies up in each Battalion, in extended order, with one company and HQ Company in support. All companies were involved, and would advance as one, over a distance of about a mile from the starting line. Bayonets were fixed and on the signal from Sporran everyone moved under cover of the guns, aircraft and smoke. Our tactical HQ – consisting of the CO, myself, signal officer and intelligence officer – and the defence platoon moved about 200 yards behind the leading troops and tanks.

We had gone about a furlong when the CO shouted, 'God, they're dropping,' and true enough, one could see the troops dropping to the ground, but only momentarily. I got my field glasses on them and realized that they were not being killed or wounded, but stooping down to pick tomatoes that were growing in the field over which we were advancing. I was told to signal the commanders to keep their troops advancing and never mind the tomatoes (*kyengendas* in Burmese). Whether or not the troops got the message, the advance went inexorably on, the bayonets glinting in the sun.

After the war, a Japanese general is reported as having said that the sight of this unending line of British bayonets advancing on his troops was the most terrifying and unnerving experience that he had ever known. The Japanese, however, did not run away, and soon our troops came under fire from the positions hidden in the thick jungle country we were leading up to. Smoke was put down, the pace quickened and in went the infantry with the tanks in close support – with various degrees of support. By noon all positions along the front had been taken and the pursuit went on to prevent further enemy consolidation: by two o'clock we were in possession of Ava Bridge, and lunch was brought up. A halt was declared and we settled down to consolidate our position, because it would not be long before the engineers would be moving up to carry out temporary repairs to the bridge.

The work of the Royal Engineers throughout had been most impressive, even spectacular. In the early days, at Kohima, they had built ramps up to the Japanese bunkers, in the face of heavy fire, to enable tanks to be winched up to fire into the very fire slits of the bunkers, as they were so strongly built. When the break out to Imphal started, and continued along the road, the Engineers converted the track into a reasonable road, and built and repaired bridges so that even heavy vehicles could move freely, for this was the only lifeline the army had. When we came to the Chindwin the REs floated a pontoon bridge out of a creek and swung it right across the river to provide a crossing for men, animals and all types of vehicles. The crossing of the Irrawaddy was greatly facilitated by their efforts, and when a bridgehead had been established it was not long ere jetties and runways for aircraft were in operation.

We were resting in the village near Ava when the Headman came to the CO and invited him and me to a celebration feast at his *basha*, or house. That night we went over to his wooden (teak) bungalow where he and his top men were waiting to receive us, sitting cross-legged in a circle. The preliminaries gone through, the food – consisting mainly of chicken with rice and a wide range of vegetables – was brought in by the women, in large metal bowls. Goodness knows where he got the provender, because the whole countryside was devastated by war, and animals of any kind were very scarce. We were given metal plates and helped ourselves to the *cana* (food): we were pressed to pile it higher and higher on our plates. Then the rice wine came in, and it took the form of a rice brew in a bamboo container with a small bamboo tube to suck the liquor from. This was kept going by pouring boiling water onto the fermenting rice and sucking. Strangely enough a cool drink oozed from it. Everybody got merrier and merrier, and by the time we decided to go, we were all very happy. We had of course taken the precaution of having a couple of guards with us but they also had a feast outside the room, while keeping an eye on us. The Burmese were pleased to see us and were glad to be rid of the unspeakable Japs.

The battle for Mandalay was now on. It would not be easy, for the terrain was intersected by canals, roads and the railway line, but soon we were on the move and each day saw a minor skirmish of one kind or other. The ring of steel round the old capital was closing in and it would be a question of capitulation or slipping out in the night through any gaps that might still be left open. This was what they did, by filtering out by night into the plain of Burma.

While we were moving in on Mandalay we had a visit from the Supremo, Lord Louis Mountbatten, who was going round the units in his jeep. He had suffered severe damage to his eye which had been pierced by a sliver of bamboo. He wore a patch on one eye but was his usual jocular self and appeared to be scenting the smell of victory as his armies gathered momentum. Mandalay fell and we entered from the south and west. The buildings were flattened and so was the Palace of the Kings of Burma, which was built of wood and stood on an island surrounded by a moat. It was said that there was a tunnel under the moat to the palace and that this had facilitated the Japanese escape. We consolidated our positions and I spent a few hours searching the grounds of the palace but did not find a crown or a peacock throne of gold.

One afternoon Alan Roy, who was 2/1C, organized a small party of officers to visit the hill town of Maymyo which was a holiday centre in the days of the British. Maymyo lay about 50 miles to the north-east of Mandalay and was reached by a narrow, winding road climbing all the way. When we emerged in the town at the top, before us lay a most beautiful lake: the colour of the waters were a mixture of blue, green and purple, and made a most dramatic effect on the mind after the unending jungles and deserts. There was little in the bazaars but a few trinkets which we tried to buy with the sort of money we had. There was also a very beautiful English church undamaged but entirely denuded of furniture. We could not stay long but were able to gaze over into China while we ate a bite of lunch. The roads were subject to Japanese patrol activity, so back we went. The CO, who hadn't come with us, was not at all amused and administered individually a mild rocket for taking ourselves so far outside the Battalion sphere of activity. But he wasn't too well and had to take to his tent for most of the time with a temperature. Alan

Roy had to take over command for the move south into the dry belt.

Soon we were held up in the middle of the driest and hottest place imaginable. The temperature was 120 degrees Fahrenheit, and the opposition was in an elevated village area surrounded by great boulders. Carriers were sent out to reconnoitre but came under heavy fire and had to be rescued. In the box of one of the carriers was a hen, providing a steady supply of eggs for the crew. In no way could the carrier be abandoned so a formal attack was laid on by Alan on the village among the rocks. Everything was organized, with tanks right up front with the infantry. I was standing beside Alan, watching the advance, when he said, 'What the hell's that behind the leading tank?' With the aid of glasses I diagnosed the Company truck, with its 21/C Captain Haworth Price on board, with the company dinner all steaming hot, ready for serving after the battle. Off we went after them and were able to join them for lunch after the capture of the village had been completed. Such was the blasé approach to the battle, and the routine now achieved after months of combat. The attention to the men's material and spiritual needs was ever a feature of the regiment all through the campaign.

We were always sorry when comrades left the Battalion and I was particularly so when Willie McKillop – 'Willie J' as he was called – went off to Delhi on a staff job. He was anxious to marry his fiancée, who had come out to Delhi in the medical corps, and this was our way of giving WJ and Cupid a push in the right direction. They were married some weeks later.

For the rest of us it was still shot and shell and all movement was in a southerly direction, clearing all before us on a wide front down the Irrawaddy banks. The main

Japanese army, however, was now holding the Mektila area, in the centre of Burma, and Slim had sent a fresh army corps right across our front to rout them out. Our advance had to stop to let this great force cross our path; and what a sight it was! There were tanks, trucks, guns and a plethora of other vehicles all with pennants flying in the sunshine. Marching infantry formations accompanied them, including the Gurkhas moving at high speed; the Sikhs with their beards and turbans; the Maharattas; the Punjabis; the Dogras; the Scots with their pipes and long strides; as well as the English county regiments. Such a sight had not been seen since the days of Kubla Khan and it is doubtful if it will ever be seen again. I would hope not, anyway.

When the dust had settled, off we went again and I suppose the sight of the 33 Corps crashing south was just as impressive; the difference was, of course, that we were forged in the heat of battle for nearly a year now. Our target was now Myingyan, a port of the Irrawaddy. The heat in the plains was now terrific, sometimes well over 100°, and men were beginning to flag. It was around this area that the trade in 'precious' stones took place. It was the part of Burma where the ruby mines were and from time to time one was approached by a native offering to barter a stone for butter, bacon, salt or pretty nearly any type of food. Many jewels were acquired to be hidden away in pockets, eventually to take their proud place on engagement rings. I acquired quite a nice hoard only to have them stolen later by a suspect servant.

There were also peddlers of less desirable merchandise than rubies. This was palm toddy, or *arak* as it was more popularly known, a powerful form of alcoholic drink that produced blindness and even death when over-indulged. Sadly some of our men suffered from both. In many cases it was difficult to determine whether the fatality was due to drinking *arak* or to snake bite for the latter was always a possibility especially with the poisonous *krait* always around.

The fight for Myingyan was taken in our stride, with the usual tactical approach on two fronts, and when we dug in we ensured that we were as near as possible to the river so that a well-earned swim could be enjoyed. Such activity, however, had to be indulged under supervision and proper protection, for in this war no position was entirely safe from attack from behind or from the flanks, as well as from the legitimate front. Myingyan was in line with Mektila so that when the latter fell the northern part of Burma would now be in our hands, including the oil-producing areas of Chauk and Yenangyaung.

We were now approaching one of the most extraordinary geographical features of central Burma. The great plain stretches from north to south and is mainly unrelieved flatness, but suddenly there is a 5,000 foot pillar, rising up from the desert. It is a burnt-out volcano and is called Mount Popa. It is a mysterious place, an ancient place of pilgrimage for the kings of Burma and, as far as we were concerned, a Japanese stronghold, for it was pitted with caves and strewn with boulders, all of which provided excellent cover for the defender and, as we were soon to discover, gave shelter for the enemy guns: they were hidden in the caves, pushed out to fire a few rounds, then pulled back into the caves to prevent damage from counter battery fire. We could see this feature from 50 miles away.

The other feature of the Burmese countryside was of course the pagoda. The Burmese pagoda is cone-shaped, circular and painted white: near the top are bells which are really round, flat, coin-like objects which are suspended so that they tinkle constantly in the breeze. The pagodas are generally constructed of stone or brick and have a low rectangular entrance which leads by a tunnel of similar size to the chamber which is also circular in shape and has a dome of about seven foot high at the apex, containing the image of the Buddha. When the situation was relatively quiet we would put our kit in there and sleep very comfortably in the interior.

On one occasion we halted in an area where there were several pagodas. I said to MacDougal, 'Put my kit into the pagoda, and yours too.' His reply was, 'I'm no going into that "padoga", it's full of boogie traps.' He may not have been right on this occasion but quite clearly the Japs were adept at setting booby traps as they retreated, to catch the unwary entering a building or hut for the first time. The outcome on this occasion was that we made alternative arrangements for our overnight accommodation by digging the usual slit trench.

As we approached Popa, news came that we were being taken out of the battle zone. We had fought manfully for a long time and were tired. We had marched hundreds of miles, crossed mountains, traversed great forests and passed over rivers. In spite of reinforcements our numbers were now very low. Nervertheless we could still carry out whatever task was required of us and would continue to do so until withdrawn from the fray. This was welcome news, so on we went to Mount Popa, the home of the Hamadryad, or the King Cobra as he was more commonly known. We soon found that the enemy were there in force. The taking of it would be a difficult task but it was a task that we would be spared for another formation could take over and we would be pulled out.

Then the whole Battalion was ordered to converge on a

point, where a general from Army staff stood with our own Divisional Commander, General Nicholson, who introduced the visitor. The latter told us that unfortunately the formation which was to relieve us would not be available and that it was now necessary for us to go forward and take Mount Popa to clear the enemy out, and then hopefully we would be relieved. he appreciated that we had done a magnificent job, and were now tired, but our spirits were high and would call on this extra effort in the true tradition of the British Army. It is customary for three cheers to be called for on such occasions but I cannot recollect any cheers raised by the listeners.

I had to settle down and prepare battle orders, on the instructions of Sporran who had now recovered from his malaise. We were constantly being harassed by enemy gunfire. The plan was to advance over boulder-strewn country, against the enemy, then push on upwards into the mountain, clearing pockets of resistance as we went. For this battle we were to have the support of the Inverness Battery of Heavy Ack-Ack, firing in a ground role from several miles back. Furthermore, we were to be visited by American generals and members of their press.

On the morning in question the Brass Hats arrived and were dispersed among our forward troops so that they might have a front-seat view of the proceedings. We dug ourselves into shallow holes just to keep the target as low as possible and waited for the big guns from away back. They came all right but did not drop on the enemy positions; they dropped all around us. The Americans had been very blasé up until now, but they soon started to scrape away at the hard earth with fingers and borrowed bayonets, to lower the profile. As the guns were not under command of the Division, so the request for lifting the fire had to be channelled back to Army, then forward to the Ack-Ack. This process took about ten minutes; in all, one of the longest ten minutes in one's life. However, they eventually got on to the target, together with our own guns, which were up to their usual standard of perfection. When the dust had settled, the objectives were taken, and the Americans left most impressed, though a little shaken.

As we made our way up the mountain, skirmishing, we found guns and equipment hidden in the caves, but what struck us most was the strangeness and eeriness of the place. Great black rock boulders stood everywhere and there was always the wall of rock itself, towering upwards to the sky. The views were breathtaking, out over the plains, and it was pleasant to find some shade and some relief from the torrid heat so far below.

We would have liked to linger, but the order went out to move off the mountain and embus for Myingyan whence we would fly out of Burma. The relief was enormous, but for me it was hard work. First of all, I had to arrange the convoy of lorries and then the pay loads of troops and equipment for the Dakota aircraft to fly back to India. All this, however, we did, for the Battalion HQ team was efficient and could meet any emergency, whether it was sited in a bunker, a tent, a *basha*, a cave, a flea-ridden hut, or a deserted palace or temple. We had a typewriter and a duplicator, a barrack-room table and a blanket and a few chairs. All of these were essential to the smooth running of the Battalion. The signaller of my former platoon saw to our communication so that liaison with the companies and outward to the higher echelons was always available by line or radio.

Chapter Ten

As we trundled along the track to the airstrip other formations were moving along in the opposite direction and on
the same road. The exchange of greetings between us and
the troops going into action were a treat to hear, for the
army folklore that exists between regiments doesn't always
include a great deal of respect, one for the other. For instance, at that time the Guards Regiments did not go further
afield than Egypt. A member of a line regiment talking about
a scarce commodity would use the expression 'As scarce as
a Guardsman's shit in India'.

Even out of the line danger lurks. I was in a jeep behind
a lorry-load of Jocks, who were sitting on the sides, looking
inwards; the equipment on their backs stuck out. Suddenly,
an oncoming lorry of troops came very close and ripped off
a grenade which landed on the bonnet of our jeep. I saw it
coming and noticed that the hand grip had sprung open.
As it landed I grabbed it and flung it to the left, just over a
bank, where it went off, not injuring anyone – as far as we
knew.

We reached Myingyan and set up bivouacs for the night
by the airstrip, where dozens of planes were lined up.
Carrying out my Adjutant duties, I saw each plane load up,
together with the QM, Alec Leckie. Ours would be the last
to leave. There was a snag, however. The CSM of HQ
Company, who was one of the bravest warriors, was dead
scared to fly. There was of course no option, but we all got

in and two people sat very close to him, chatting all the time, telling him to close his eyes while we took off along the bumpy airstrip, and into the clear air. We looked down on the mountains we had marched over and could scarcely believe that they were so high. We sat on seats along each side of the plane, grasping our weapons, ashen faced, and as the plane bobbed down in air pockets we hoped that the journey would soon be over.

Suddenly it was bump, bump and we were down. The place was Chittagong, which had been one of the key bases for the campaign in the Arakan. It is an important river port and centre of communications, but in those days not on the railway. To get to the rail head we had to board a river steamer and sail northwards for a few hours. This was very pleasant, because of the warm weather, but also the only cargo on board appeared to be cases of Indian gin, Mariners by name, and a great mound of coconuts on deck. We were able to purchase the gin very cheaply but there was no tonic water to go with it. Someone thought of the coconut milk and there was the perfect answer: gin and coconut milk. The warriors lay back on deck and swilled their novel concoction, while the jungle and the crocodiles slid by. We ate our hard rations and broke out into song, then fell asleep.

Eventually we came to a jetty, close to the rail terminus where a train was waiting to take us to Calcutta. We had been travelling all day, and no sooner had we consumed a hot meal on the station platform, plus a mug of *char*, than we got on board and fell into a dreamless sleep, to awaken with the train passing through paddy fields with what seemed to be water everywhere. For we were now in the Ganges delta and nearing our destination which we reached during the morning.

In true army style we boarded lorries straight away,

which trundled us up a dusty road, out of the great sprawling city of Calcutta, up the river to a camp some 30 miles away at Bandel. Here was peace and a taste of civilian life.

All around us were jute mills, managed by Scots from the jute capital of Dundee. Hospitality from their fellow Scots was plentiful and it was here that I contacted my old friend Addie Brown who was in the RAF photographic interpretation section. We played golf and visited friends and presently, with Dave Davison and Ian Swanson, arranged a leave to Kalimpong, far up in the Himalayas, not far from the towering heights of Kunchenjunga. This was a great adventure to be free after months of conflict. I had been promoted to Major just before leaving Burma, and was pleased to enjoy the privileges which go with field rank.

Off we went by train, heading north into the foothills where the line branches off, left to Darjeeling and right on a miniature ratchet line, up the steep mountain to Kalimpong. I was sent off in front, while the rest organized the luggage, catching a train that was leaving straight away: on arrival I would carry out a recce and arrange suitable accommodation. The journey is quite hair-raising because of the steepness and the precipices which border the line, but you reach the little station in good order, among an excited crowd of Indians of all kinds, mixed with Nepalese, Bhutanese, Tibetans and warriors from Sikkhim.

I got myself a horse-drawn *gharry* and explained to the driver what my requirements were, suggesting that a Dak bungalow might be suitable. No sooner said than done. We arrived at a Dak bungalow, which is a feature of the Indian scene. These bungalows are provided by the government, in the less accessible areas, for the convenience of travellers. They have the essential furnishings and a staff to manage the place. This one had sufficient amenity for our needs, as well as a magnificent view of the mountains, and it was within easy distance of the town and one of the local hotels. I duly hired the place and returned to the station to await the arrival of my mates.

They did eventually arrive, in no fit state, but I had by now secured a taxi which was capable of taking all four of us, plus all the gear which consisted of the bed rolls and a few cases containing the necessary clothing for the holiday. On arrival, everyone expressed his satisfaction with the arrangements and, after a preliminary drink, we went off to bed until hunger awoke us from our slumbers.

We called for the *kitmagar*, the *bhisti* and the *bobajee*. In the event the *kitmagar* was sent down to the hotel to order a meal, the *bhisti* got the baths going and the *bobajec* was given instructions as to future meals, the purchase of food from the bazaar and so on. We hadn't anything very much for the *mali* (the gardener) but he assured us that he had a brother who was a *cyce* (a horse man) who would bring four horses round in the morning for the sahibs to ride. Things were beginning to take shape and, after bathing and dressing, the sun was going down and the *kitmagar* – and, by now, a *chokra* (boy) – were standing by to pour out the drinks which we had brought anyway.

The hotel was owned and run by people who claimed they were Scots, like us, although perhaps other races had made a contribution to their present condition. The meal was superb and when it was all over the gramophone came out and dancing to the records ensued, although the female representation was very scarce indeed. The party was continued at the bungalow and when the *cyce* appeared with the horses next morning we were not really ready, although in due course we mounted and moved off in somewhat irregular order, with the horses seeming to decide where we should go. They were really ponies rather like the High-land Garron, and gave you a very comfortable ride with a minimum of posting. They were also sure footed on narrow tracks, and didn't mind heights.

One day we all went to Darjeeling; a much more sophis-ticated town and at a lower level of the Himalayas. While Bill and Addie went sketching, Ian and I took a taxi up the mountains to visit the famous Kalimpong schools. These are residential schools, founded and run by the Church of Scot-land for the care and education of Anglo-Indian children; and very well run they were by a dedicated band of Scots teachers and workers. The schools covered a wide area, and included a farm which was a model of efficiency, producing much of the food for the children and staff. The children lived in small houses, overseen by a house mother, and no happier community could one find anywhere. There was a pond full of the lotus flower, and at the highest point were the graves of the founder Doctor Graham and his wife. The scenery all around was breathtaking and included, in the late afternoon, a sight of the snow-capped peak of Kunchen-junga. We were sorry to leave this place and take the hair-raising drive back to Kalimpong.

In our absence the other two had organized a sort of safari or trek into Bhutan and Sikkhim leading up to the borders of Tibet. We were well equipped for this as we had our bedding. We hired an old American car, the driver of which was our guide, and went off into the mountains, and for three days we walked, drove and rode ponies on bridle tracks to Tibetan monasteries and native villages. Every-where along the tracks were prayer wheels and narrow prayer flags fluttering in the breeze. The air at nearly 10,000 feet was clear and refreshing, and beyond that height one was aware of an increasing rarefication. The alpine flowers in the meadows brightened the scene. The people were friendly and smiling. In Bhutan they were tall, fierce-looking men with long, black, highly-embroidered, skirt-like garments and carrying wicked-looking knives at their belts. They wore Cossack-style hats in the same material as the clothing. High boots into which the trousers were squeezed completed the costume: very dignified and suitable for the occasion.

We climbed, with the help of mules and our own feet, quite a bit up the slopes of Kunchenjunga, but neither the time or the equipment justified going further than about 18–20,000 feet. We returned to our Dak bungalow happy with our experiences and were soon making plans for the descent to the plains, and the hot, humid atmosphere of the Calcutta area.

No sooner had we returned than the signal came that the war in Europe had ended and there were celebrations everywhere. It was, of course, academic for us who were standing by to go back in to Burma or Malaya by a seaborne landing.

Addie Brown invited me over to his RAF mess for their victory party. It was as hilarious as these occasions are: I was standing at the bar in the uniform of a Highland officer of field rank, when an RAF junior officer appeared with a bucket of water, which he emptied over me. In a flash I drew my *sgian dhu* from my stocking and gave chase. He ran like mad and disappeared round the corner of the veranda. In the dark I didn't see this and, with a great dash, went straight over the veranda rail and dropped six feet into a lily pond which cooled me off considerably as I struck out for the bank, my *sgian dhu* still clutched tightly in my fist.

By now the rest of the party were gazing over the rail into the limpid waters of the pond. I was soaked and a kilt is a very difficult garment to dry. The RAF CO was furious to know who had committed this dastardly offence against a visitor. I never knew what transpired but resumed the party and arrived back in camp in the early hours happy with my night's adventure.

Games and sports took up a lot of our time, as well as practising driving jeeps over rough ground, for it appeared that when we went on our next foray from the sea we would have lots of these wonderful machines to speed our advance inland. There were also visits to jute mills with much hospitality. One of these mills had the largest fly wheel in the world and very impressive it was.

A feature of our stay at Bandel was that to get to it from Calcutta one had to pass through a small French territory called Chandranagore. It was open to the British, and we suspected that some of the troops took advantage of the French customs during our stay there!

Soon, however, we moved to better-known territory some 50 miles from our beloved Secunderabad, at a tented camp at Kamareddi. Here we started to receive an influx of reinforcements and quite a number of new officers joined us, proud to join a regiment, the fame of whose exploits in Burma had spread far and wide: they now wanted nothing more than for the Battalion to return to the fray. In the mean time there were many postings out of the Battalion of experienced senior officers, all with temporary promotions to staff jobs all over India. Then my time came. I had been selected to go down to Bombay to help train the new armies coming out from Europe. I had never been posted out of the First Battalion since joining it in 1941. It was now 1945 so the parting was quite a thought. The reward, of course, was the rank of Lieutenant Colonel.

The night before my departure the CO gave a special dinner in my honour and a very special night it was. Friends from other units were invited and whisky and Athol Brose flowed. The pipers played and the occasion was graced with the presence of the Pipe Major, Euan Macrae, who was the youngest in the Army at the time. He hailed from Skye, so was a fellow country man of my own. The subalterns' four was danced in the form of a Highland Reel and the Argyle Broadswords was danced by four drummers. There were speeches when the CO proposed my health and called for the toast to be drunk with Highland honours which meant that instead of drinking the toasts standing on the floor, all got up on their chairs, put one foot on the table, swallowed the dram and dropped the glasses over their shoulders. Some of them survived while others crashed in a thousand pieces.

Next day was Sunday and departure of myself and batman MacDougal was scheduled for after lunch. A large number of friends from other units again converged on the mess to bid us Godspeed. After lunch we were led out of the mess to a 15-cwt truck, to the front of which was attached two long ropes. The officers, WOs and sergeants took up the ropes, the pipe band took its place in front and, as far as the eye could see in front, both sides of the road were lined by soldiers. We did not sit but stood on the seat as the roof was open, and as the pipe band struck up and marched off we waved in acknowledgement of the cheering Jocks who had been our companions for all these years, in and out of battle. The officers pulled on the ropes and the procession went along like this to the station which was just under a mile away.

The train took us through the tropical night to Bombay, whence we were transported in the usual manner of the Army to a camp and allocated our quarters. I found my way to the mess and, after drinks, sat down to the evening meal. We were all strangers but the talk was of a big bomb, some claimed to call it an atom bomb, having been dropped on Japan. We had no idea of its effect or implications – only that it was a big bomb and not to be compared with ordinary big bombs that had been dropped on cities all over the world during the last six years. Then there was a rumour that a second one of these things had been dropped and then the greatest of all rumours – that the Japs had capitulated. A day later it was all official. An atom bomb had been dropped on Hiroshima and Nagasaki, and the Japanese had surrendered.

There was great rejoicing; but what about my job as instructor in jungle warfare to the new armies coming out from England? We were all asking the same question, and there was no answer, except that all the plans had been abandoned. There was nothing for us to do but to rejoin our units, so back went MacDougal and I to Kamareddi camp. My job had been taken over by another; I wasn't even a major any more, far less a lieutenant colonel! Back I went to my substantive rank of captain and was sent up to Division, to see what they could do for me. They were terribly sorry, old boy, jolly bad luck, etc., back you go to the Battalion and we'll see what turns up!

In the army something does, for next day the newly vacant office of OC, HQ Company was offered to me and I was back in business again with full field rank. Such was the rapid movement of officers now that after a few weeks I found myself in command of the Battalion, notwithstanding that it was in a very temporary capacity.

I arranged a football match with the Nizam of Hyderabad's state forces. The great day came and the whole Battalion went down to Secunderabad in trucks and duly took their place with the locals round the pitch. I was seated beside His Excellency and in came the two teams who gave a breathtaking display of their respective interpretations of the game. On the one hand the Glasgow-dominated Cameron side, with their clever dribbling, heading and short passes, while on the Indian side were the long passes and the swift rushes for interception. We won in the end and there were refreshments for the troops while the officers were regaled with food and drink and, as a special treat, shown some of the strong rooms loaded with jewels, for the Nizam was the richest man in the world.

In true military fashion we all, officers and men, returned home together in the convoy as we had come, moving out of Hyderabad to the music of the Nizam's military band. As usual, some had opted to stay behind and enjoy the blandishments of Hyderabad city. They were duly returned to camp and dealt with. Shortly after this, Major Jock Makgill Chrichton arrived from overseas and took command, and I returned to the command of HQ Company.

Secunderabad was some 30 miles away, and we were given the oversight of a camp on the racecourse there. It was put under my command as OC HQ Company, and this necessitated visiting the camp from time to time at frequent intervals to take company orders and other administrative and disciplinary matters. But the war was over, and thoughts of home dominated all our minds.

There was much movement within the Battalion, in and out, and soon it became clear that there was a new Battalion forming, when it was announced that the Camerons would represent Scotland in the Commonwealth formation proceeding to the occupation of Japan. This was a matter of pride, for it was made known that the honour was a reward for their magnificent performance in the recent campaign. It was clear, however, that few of the warriors who had fought their way from Kohima to Rangoon would see Japan. They would be repatriated and a mainly new Battalion would go to Japan. This was brought about by a move of the old hands to Deolali, near Bombay. We still maintained our companies and lower formations but we were now the First Cameron repatriates, awaiting the boat to bring us home to Blighty.

Chapter Eleven

We took advantage of the leisure time by getting ourselves kitted out in Bombay for civvy street. The Indian contractors who had supplied all our needs for the past four and a half years supplied us with suits and shirts, shoes and coats at very moderate prices, in appreciation of our good custom – and it wasn't just in clothing, for the crates of Scotch and other liquors were arriving daily for our delectation. Mote Ram, Raham Bux and Wazir Ali were our friends.

I still had my personal jeep which I had 'bought' earlier on, and very useful it was in running down to Bombay to give us our final fling on the Willingdon Golf Course, the Cricket Club of India, or the Royal Yacht Club of Bombay, as well as meals in the Taj Mahal.

Then suddenly, and with little warning, it was onto the train, down to the docks and straight onto the *Winchester Castle*; a very large Union Castle Line ship converted for trooping. It was very different from the *Marnix* which had brought us here: everything was basic, and soon we found that it was dry. To our chagrin we learned that when the Americans came into the war, our troopships went dry, to conform with the Yankee practice. The Americans are a funny race: when they impose Spartan conditions on themselves they expect their friends to do likewise. However, there was always the first officer, who was usually Scots on board these ships. Once safely ensconced on board, we became friendly with him and were invited to frequent chats in his cabin on deck. I had 'sold' my jeep for a case of whisky and a few bottles of gin, so one way or another being a dry ship was no great hardship.

I shared a cabin with Ian Swanson and a major of the Worcesters. He was a strong man and an amateur weight-lifter. One night Ian and I came down to our cabin and felt in need of a drink. We didn't switch on the light because the strong man was sleeping soundly in his cot. We felt around for the bottle and two glasses and then poured out the liquor in the dark. As I drank mine I felt something slide down the glass onto my lips. What was this in the glass? I crept quietly out into the corridor, which was lit up, and there, to my surprise, in the glass were the strong man's false teeth! I returned to the cabin, placed the teeth on a shelf and resumed our quiet but hilarious little session, before turning in.

We stopped off at Aden to refuel and held a concert in the harbour. It was stifling hot and the piper played a very well-known tune, *The Barren Rocks of Aden*. One of our senior officers was heard to ask what tune the piper was playing and when told, replied, 'The barren rocks of what?'

The sail through the canal and bitter lake was at night, but it was well worth while leaning over the rail watching the changing scene in the moonlight. Palm trees, Bedouin tents, towns and Arab coastal craft: all very romantic and reminiscent of Ali Baba and the Arabian Nights.

It was 11 November, Armistice Day, and the ship's company decided to celebrate as well as commemorate. At eleven o'clock a religious service was held on deck with all members of the ship's complement present. We remembered our fallen and looked back over the past five years and all that they had meant to us and the world. The Nazis had tried to dominate the Western World and after a Titanic struggle were forced to surrender, bringing freedom to the fettered and peace to millions in conflict. We had lost friends and comrades and had given our own blood and youthful energy. Would the world be grateful? It was said that we who had halted the other tyranny of the Eastern World, Japan, were the 'forgotten army'. There were many conflicting thoughts as we sung *Oh God Our Help in Ages Past* in sight of the Nile.

In the afternoon a great race meeting was held: programmes and a tote made the scene more realistic and those who had some connection with the turf acted as bookmakers as well. The names and genealogy of the horses were as pornographic as the combined efforts of a victorious army on their way home could devise. Money was lost and won, but money never seemed to be of much importance. In the evening there was a banquet, with music and high jinks, as we sailed up the Mediterranean.

When we awoke in the morning the ship was tossing in the most almighty storm. I went up to breakfast and, on entering the dining saloon, saw only about six there instead of several hundred. The passageway between the tables was nearly vertical; down one minute, then vertical up the next. However, I got a good breakfast inside me, as did the valiant few, and the storm raged all day and the next night. The morning found us at rest, but in the shelter of the harbour of Valetta in Malta, for outside the storm still raged, and we were told that St Paul had been shipwrecked on this island of Melita (now Malta) and no wonder if the storm was anything like what it was now. Soon we were on our way again, and in fair weather, passing through the Straits of Gibraltar out into the Atlantic: but we were nearing home now and this was all that mattered, for it could only be a few days.

We awoke one morning and, looking through the port-hole, saw the most spectacular sight we had seen for years and years – green fields. We ran up on deck and there they were: the green fields of the Isle of Wight, for we were approaching Southampton. Green like this was something we had forgotten in the barrenness of the eastern lands.

Soon we had stopped: our odyssey was over and, as the tug eased us towards the harbour, we could see a woman with a red scarf walking and waving on the jetty. Tears came to our eyes and we realized we were crying. As the ship tied up the whole company lined the gunnels. There was obviously a reception party – complete with platform, red carpet, flags, loudspeakers and microphones. We strained to see if we could recognize any of the party. Soon a cheer went up, for among those present was General Grover who had led us through to our first ever victory, over the Japs at Kohima and was then sent home. The CIGS started to speak and was given a hearing for a few minutes, then the call went up, 'We want Grover', in an increasing crescendo until the top man had to give way to General Grover. He was back among his own soldiers who listened with intensity to his every word of welcome and praise for what they had done for him, for their country and for the world. When it was all over a roar went up; bush hats were waved and flung in the air, some never to find the same head again.

We moved from the ship to the station where eventually we met up with our gear which we had brought with us from India to be dealt with by the customs: but the customs officers were good; they knew that in these bundles and packages were the spoils of war and this was not the occasion for embarrassment. There were swords, knives, rifles, mortars, uniforms, flags, jewels and saris, all destined for crofts, flats, houses and farms all over Scotland, and the rest of the United Kingdom as well.

Everything and every place seemed dull and dilapidated as we moved northward in the train, and we still didn't know our destination. It was as if we were still at war. The train travelled slowly and there were many stops. It was winter with snow and ice everywhere and as evening of the next day fell we were approaching the Scottish border and a cheer went up an hour or so later as we passed slowly through Edinburgh. There were no more halts and by midnight the snow-clad Highland hills were all around.

I knew the form well for I had traversed it countless times: we had crossed Drumochter, run down to Newtonmore, Kingussie and Aviemore, pushing on to the Slochd to run down to Inverness – home, but still no stop! On, on, until three in the morning, we came to a grinding halt in Strathpeffer. The platform was open to the sky and was a solid path of ice as was the road we traversed to the Spa Hotel, which appeared to be a wartime HQ for that part of the Highlands. The CO who had met us at the station was a Cameron and he gave a warm welcome to us in the mess where there was whisky and tea with sandwiches before dropping into beds. He would speak to us at eleven in the morning. This he did on the upstairs landing of the mess.

He told us how proud the regiment was of our deeds and that we would have six weeks' leave before reporting back to Edinburgh for duty, for most of us were still to remain in the colours for many months to come. A special train would be leaving later to take us to our destinations as far as Edinburgh and Glasgow and then onward to London. So it was back on a train, for I was rejoining my wife Ada in Edinburgh. That journey down to Edinburgh was the last occasion we were to be together as officers of the

First Battalion Cameron Highlanders who had soldiered
together through thick and thin for over five years. We knew
each other very well and were to be friends for the rest of
our lives.

Chapter Twelve

The reunion with Ada was warm and loving and soon it was as if the years of separation had never been. Next day was Saturday and we walked in Princes Street in the morning and met innumerable friends in and out of uniform. There was an officers' club in Princess Street. We drifted in; the piano was being played. I recognized the player as Bill Dallas. I stepped up behind him and started to sing *Kishmuls Galley*. He changed to the accompaniment and everybody gathered around: we were home. We caught a train for Inverness and back we went into the bosom of the family.

Mam was there as competent as ever, Auntie as busy as ever and Jock singing his Gaelic songs. Grandfather had gone and although he had escaped participation in wars he had a military-type funeral for, on that day and for a few days before, his farm at Drumbuie had been occupied by hundreds of soldiers on manoeuvres. They carried the coffin to the hearse and lined the route to the cemetery. The rest of the relations were in good form and my brother Will had been released from his prisoner-of-war camp in Poland and had come home to get married.

I visited the local hostelry with Uncle Alec and no jollier night could be imagined among the folk I knew so well. There was a good deal of boasting and bragging and the Gaelic flowed with the whisky. I soon realized that the civilian population were living on very strict rations, although in the Highlands this was not so apparent, for it could always be supplemented from the local land, air and water. Whisky was in fair supply but beer was short, although here again the shortages manifested themselves more in the cities than in the country. It was an occasion for jollity, however, and there were ceilidhs everywhere and we spent our evenings being entertained and entertaining. The community gave a function, in the Public Hall, for the returned service men and women, presenting them with a welcome home certificate, and a sum of money in grateful appreciation of their efforts.

One day I received a communication from the War Office, which was to have an important repercussion on my whole future. I was a teacher and would return on demobilization to my post in Kirkcaldy. This communication said that emergency training colleges were being set up by the government to provide ex-service people with crash courses for teacher-training in order to make up the enormous deficit caused by the war. If I were interested in applying for a lectureship in one of these colleges in England, I should do so on the form provided. I did so and thought no more of the matter, for soon we were back in Edinburgh reporting to Scottish command for a posting.

There I met my colleagues of Burma, recalled for the same purpose. I went in and was greeted by a magnificent staff officer who asked me what I would like to do with my remaining six months in the Army. Did I want Germany? No. Well, what about Liaison Officer with the Polish Army in Scotland? Yes. So I was appointed as Major, General Staff Liaison with the Second Polish Corps. My knowledge of Polish was negligible, but the Army doesn't worry much about these things.

My first posting was to the HQ Polish Liaison in Edinburgh itself. There was a mixture of Polish and British officers. One of my jobs was to assist in the arrangements for transferring the whole corps from the south of Scotland to the north by rail, another was to interview aggrieved husbands of wives who were believed to be having affairs with Poles. The latter must have wondered what special qualifications they had for being suddenly posted to the Shetland Islands. There were many other tasks of a more confidential nature to undertake and I applied myself to learning a few useful phrases.

Soon I too was posted north where the troops had gone. First I found myself in Broughty Ferry, with the job of carrying out an inventory of ammunition dumps all over this wide region. It meant interviewing landowners who had kindly given the facility to erect dumps during the war. These aristocratic gentlemen were very hospitable and it was on more than one occasion that I was glad that I had a driver to drive me back to my billet in Broughty. I was beginning to get to know the Poles and was a frequent member of their officers' messes. The young officers were now speaking English quite fluently and had a mind to remain in this country and create a new life here. The older men, colonels and generals had no interest in learning English or in making a new life for themselves.

One of the problems in their camps, which worried the British Medical Officer, was the sanitary standards which were so much lower than those in the British Army. He maintained that their latrines were truly 'shit houses'.

The soldiers were very good with their hands and artistic as well. They would make you shoes, shirts, suits, cigarette lighters and cases, jewellery and gadgets for the home. They were also competent mechanics and electricians.

Being in golfing country I was able to indulge myself in that great Scottish pastime and for the first time in over six years got into a pair of plus fours to sally out on the links.

As I said, I inspected camps, and on one occasion I arrived at a camp near a village at about 8 o'clock in the morning. First there were no sentries on the gates, nor was there any sign of movement within the camp which consisted of a series of huts. I went up to the first of these huts, opened the door and went in, to find all the beds occupied; and not just by a soldier to a bed but by a female as well in many of them. Everybody woke up and they were surprised to see a British officer in their midst. For the next ten minutes it was pandemonium, for I made much of the situation. Sergeants and sergeant majors were summoned and came. Where was the officer commanding? He had gone to town, the previous night, and couldn't be found. I had the women sent back to the village, got everyone on parade, harangued the sergeant major and told him to drill his sleepy troops for an hour, while I went through the camp in detail.

My next posting was to Invergordon, celebrated for its connection with the fleet. Here I found a Polish camp on the outskirts of the town. I had been driven north by a Polish driver who went through every red light on the road and could not be spoken to because he had no English and would not understand my remonstrances in pidgin Polish. I was greeted into the mess by the colonel commanding in the splendid uniform of the Polish cavalry; the cap with square, flat top like a mortar board. I was introduced to the officers, who clicked their heels. I duly bowed and was shown to my billet.

On returning to the mess for the evening meal I realized I would now be on Polish food, starting with Borscht, a soup made from beetroot, which seemed to be the starter for all main meals. But there was always a large quantity of vodka and each dram went down to the toast *nas drovia*, the equivalent of our Gaelic *slainte*. After the meal there were games of cards and dominoes and a bit of dancing, in the Russian style, to a gramophone record. I eventually took my irregular steps to my billet and realized I would have to watch this lot.

My main job here was to dispose of the barbed wire defences which ringed the coast and which the troops were busily engaged in tearing up. Where to dump this stuff was the problem. It did not appear to have any scrap value, so some of it was towed out to sea and dumped in deep holes in the sea bed, whilst the rest was put into quarries and other holes in the earth after I had persuaded the landowners to agree. This was not at all an easy job. Being in the heart of the Highlands one requirement in the approach to the landowner was a bottle of whisky, which was kept in the car and replenished frequently. Although our visits were not always productive we had no end of invitations to dinner in the evenings, for Easter Ross is a very wealthy farming area and the people were hospitable. Game was plentiful and there was always the opportunity for a shot.

I lived in the Polish camp and dined in the mess most of the time. Normally I wore the kilt, but in the camp was a sort of mascot or soldier's pet, a very large turkey cock, or Bubbly Jock as we preferred to call them. This bird seemed to have a dislike of red, for when he saw the red flashes on my hose he would attack, by pecking at my legs. As I crossed the square this attack went in as soon as I emerged from the mess and I proceeded on my way by flicking him with my ash plant. This pantomime caused great amusement for the Polish soldiers. One day, however, there had been a special lunch and great joviality, with a lot of *nas drovias*, at the end of which the CO and one or two others came to the door to see me off, although I wasn't really going anywhere. Immediately I started to walk, the attack came in and I took the usual defensive action to the great amusement of the troops who were watching. The CO saw this and gave the order in Polish to catch that bird. The order was carried out with a great flurry of feathers. The cook was fetched, the bird's neck was broken and next night he was served at table to the great jollity of everyone.

An invitation came ot me from Gloucestershire to attend for an interview for the post of lecturer in a new training college for teachers at Cheltenham: Lecturer in Mathematics. I would go, of course, but the art of mathematics and the teaching of it in six years had receded so far that it was difficult to contemplate the thought of taking my place in front of a class of students. My whole being was that of a soldier and not just a theoretical one but a practical one, living that life from day to day. Off I went, collected Ada in Edinburgh and down to Gloucester we went. There was no relaxation in the dress of the army, and as yet civilian clothes were barred to officers and men in the normal course of duty. So I turned up in the uniform with the kilt as usual, among all the chaps who were being interviewed and who came direct from their schools and colleges. There was one other in the uniform of a signals officer but he was for English studies. The panel consisted of three wise men and to my astonishment and genuine surprise I was offered and accepted the appointment. Well this was a turn-up for the book, for I was all geared up to return to my old job in Kirkcaldy and had been back there to make sure all was in order.

We went to see the college, which was residential and still in the hands of the builders, but we took the view that there was no hardship in this and it would be a challenge.

But I had better refresh my ideas about the teaching of maths before going back to Cheltenham.

On my return I was posted straight away to Inverary. GHQ were sorry that this time they could not let me have a vehicle and driver; only a motor bike! There were shortages!

First, however, I had another job to do. In Poland a new government of communist persuasion had taken over power and an agreement had been arrived at with the British government for the voluntary repatriation of Polish nationals. As a result, the service men in the Polish forces were to be given the option of returning to their native land or remaining in Britain. My role was to go to a Polish camp where the full complement of service men would be on parade, under the direct control of the camp Commandant. When all was ready, I would walk onto the parade ground accompanied by an officer of the Polish forces of similar rank. I would read the document which had come from the Foreign and War Offices in English then my opposite number would do the same in Polish. On a given command those who were opting for repatriation would take two paces forward, right turn, quick march and straight away they would be onto waiting covered army trucks: within minutes they were off. Those who wished to stay stood still looking to their front and were dismissed only after the trucks had disappeared. I did about six of these and would reckon one in three opted for repatriation. Very few really wanted to go, but their families were in Poland and they felt that they had very little option. No trouble was experienced in this very delicate exercise.

The Polish camp at Inverary was sited in the grounds of Inverary Castle, the home of the Duke of Argyle, Chief of Clan Campbell. My lodging, however, at this time was in the Argyle Arms Hotel, quite near the gates to the castle and camp. The proprietor was also the co-director of one of the leading contracting firms in Scotland and was reputedly in the millionaire class. He had built roads and aerodromes all over these islands and had earned his building expertise from years of experience and observation. He reckoned he was the dunce in his class at the village school, for he spent much of his time watching the sheep and deer winding their way up the hillsides; which told him the best way up a hill. The cleverest boy in the class had become the village postman.

From the time of my arrival I was made welcome and numerous ceilidhs were arranged for my benefit, to pass the time away in the evenings. Being a small port, it had several naval ships lying off, awaiting to be paid off. They were commanded by Lieutenant commanders who were happy to come ashore of an evening and spend the evening in the hotel. When the time for their paying off came, parties were held on board, to which I was invited. These were elaborate affairs with bands imported from towns further down Loch Fyre, and 'Gaelic choirs' from far and wide, so, apart from the food and drink, there was a large measure of entertainment as well. At the end of these festivities naval escorts saw the revellers safely ashore to places of safety.

The Poles were very helpful in my work and their camp in the grounds of the castle was a model of efficiency and activity. In the latter sense they busied themselves with manufacturing and trading goods of all description in the neighbouring countryside. The tailors made suits, shirts and coats; there were cobblers who made shoes and boots to measure; silversmiths could turn an old piece of silver into an artefact; joiners; plumbers; and mechanics. I don't suppose the local populace were served so well before or since.

My motor bike was kept in immaculate condition and although trousers were the proper wear for riding these things, more often than not I rode in the kilt, providing an enormous amount of amusement to all and sundry. One had to be careful, however, for towards evening the west of Scotland becomes a happy hunting ground for myriads of midges, flies, gnats, bees and a thousand other insects, who get into every nook and cranny of your person; a kilt on a motor bike was definitely not a suitable garment for the evening.

The Chief of Clan Campbell was an elderly bachelor and the only other inhabitants of the great and beautiful castle were a couple of equally old retainers; a cook and a butler. The Chief was very gracious. I had quite a few chats with him and was invited to afternoon tea on several occasions. His favourite garb consisted of breeches and a tartan doublet with a tweed jacket well reinforced with leather to take the strains. Of an evening he would get on his bike and cycle down to the bell tower which, most unusually for these parts, had a carillon. The tower and carillon were a memorial to all the Campbells who had lost their lives in the First World War. The Chief loved to play the carrillon and round about five in the afternoon, the trills of the bells would ring out over Loch Fyne. He was quite a performer and as good as any I've heard on the continent, particularly in Belgium.

I would arrive for tea about three in the afternoon, and be greeted by the Chief in the great hall, which houses one of the most magnificent displays of armour and weapons imaginable. Then we would move into the library which contained many priceless tomes. He was a scholar and familiar with Latin, Greek and Russian languages. At that time he had just taken possession of his late sister's library books as a legacy. The books were set out on the long oak table where they had been deposited on delivery. It would take months or years to classify them and find homes for them on the shelves. You felt that they could not have found a better and more capable custodian.

At this point the butler, who was very ancient, would indicate that tea was being served in the drawing room so we would move in there and receive tea at the hands of the butler from a silver tea service and vast tea tray, also of solid silver. Our conversation was mostly of books, authors, history and the countryside and we skilfully kept off the subject of Glen Coe. Of all the great Scottish dukes, the Campbells were possibly the most powerful and probably owned a larger section of the country than any other.

There were of course matters relating to the camp and I was able to reciprocate His Grace's hospitality in lots of ways, having the resources of some 2–3,000 men at my disposal. The fact that I was wearing a Cameron tartan kilt made no difference at that juncture, for historically the Camerons were not always the best friends of the Campbells in the old clan days.

Soon the time for my discharge from the Army came. It was now high summer in Argyle and no more beautiful spot at that time of year can be found. The hills are ablaze with colour, not just from the heather but from the wild flowers, brooms and whins that flourish in abundance there. The air is full of the scent of these blooms and the heather gives off the aroma of honey.

I had made many friends and not least among them was the hotel proprietor who, although a millionaire, was also a romantic. A week before I was due to leave I was out with him in his coach and four-in-hand which was one of his hobbies, and he told me that he was putting on a ceilidh for me to mark my stay at Inverary. I sensed this would be something big and I was not to be disappointed. The Gaels were out in force from far and near. There were singers, dancers, musicians, choirs and pipers, all in the Highland tradition. The Lochgilphead Gaelic Choir was brought up for the evening and the pipers, fiddlers, accordionists, a harpist and even a *seannachie* appeared on the scene. There was no specific starting time but people began to move in between 9 and 10 p.m. The whisky flowed and the pipers struck up and the sun had risen well over Ben Lomond before the party broke up. This is the sort of gathering that the Highlanders love, because it brings together all that is so dear to the hearts of the Gael. The singing, the music, the dance, all sustained by food and drink, enhance the good fellowship.

After a tearful farewell with my friends I bundled my kit and motorbike onto the truck which the Army authorities sent along to bring me back to HQ in Edinburgh. I had handed over to my successor who had arrived the previous night and who was able to attend the ceilidh, although he was not among those who assembled for my departure.

On arrival at Edinburgh I was given my demob papers but would have to go down to York to go through the procedure of demobilization. The journey down provided me with the opportunity of reflecting on my six years of service with His Majesty's colours. I had seen a lot in those years, had been half way around the world, had taken part in one of the most violent and arduous campaigns in the whole of military history, and I had assumed great responsibilities, which were beyond my wildest dreams as a teacher in a Fifeshire school. The most dangerous and horrendous threat to the world civilization had been removed; our generation had a great deal to be proud of. I could remember thinking as I stood or crouched in my trench on a remote hillside on the Burmese frontier clutching a sub-machine gun, that out there and beyond were the powers of darkness and barbarism, and behind me the bastions of freedom and civilization. It was on me, and countless others like me, that the responsibility for going forward or back rested so firmly.

Then I remembered my friends in the regiment. We had soldiered together for so many years, shared the fun and the dangers – and made light of the latter – swapped tales and sung songs. Would we remain friends into the future? My guess was that we would. What sort of world was I returning to? It must be different, for when we were still in India, there had been a general election and the British people had repudiated their great war leader and deliverer, Winston Churchill. Were new and different forces arising, when we were out of the country, of which we knew nothing? Time would tell.

In the mean time it was once again out of the train onto the ever-waiting truck and down to the demob centre. First a medical check-up to see what sort of condition I was in. As the doctors spoke they wrote it all down. After the medical it was over to the clothing department for a suit, a hat, coat, shoes, shirt, socks. I looked in the mirror and saw there a creature I had forgotten existed. My issue clothing and equipment were taken off me and I resumed my dress uniform, which was my own and which could be worn for another three months while I was on demobilization leave.

I caught the first train north to savour the way of life of a civilian in post-war Britain. But was it true what they said: 'Once a Cameron, always a Cameron'?

Epilogue

There is, however, a sequel to all this. In the early fifties another war broke out, this time in Korea. The United Nations went to war on the side of the South Koreans to help them defend themselves against the North Koreans. The British Government of the day decided to reform the Home Guard and I was once more embodied as an officer, albeit in the Home Guard. To begin with I served with the Gloucesters then transferred with my job to the Middlesex Regiment. We took part in the usual manoevres but paid particular attention to weapon training. In Middlesex we did our firing practice at Bisley, where we met some world-class shots. Otherwise we practised small-bore shooting on the underground ranges in London. I was a member of the team who won the Metropolitan Home Guard Cup on one occasion. At the conclusion of hostilities the Home Guard was stood down, but there were no medals!